THE PHILOSOPHY OF HISTORY

Reprint of Original Edition of 1766

VOLTAIRE

The Philosophy of History

with a Preface by Thomas Kiernan

PHILOSOPHICAL LIBRARY
New York

TO THE

MOST HIGH AND PUISSANT PRINCESS,

CATHERINE THE SECOND,

EMPRESS OF ALL THE RUSSIAS,

PROTECTRESS OF THE ARTS
AND SCIENCES,

BY HER GENIUS ENTITLED TO JUDGE
OF ANCIENT NATIONS,

AS SHE IS BY HER MERIT WORTHY
TO GOVERN HER OWN.

Humbly dedicated by the AUTHOR.

Copyright, 1965, by PHILOSOPHICAL LIBRARY, INC.
15 East 40th Street, New York 16, N. Y.

Library of Congress Catalog Card No. 65-10662

ISBN 978-0-8065-3039-1

EDITOR'S PREFACE

François Marie Arouet de Voltaire was born in Paris in 1694 and was educated at the Jesuit *College de Louis-le-Grand*. When he was 23 he spent a year in prison for allegedly being the author of insults against Philippe II, Regent of France. It was at this time that he began to call himself Voltaire and that he seriously embarked upon his career as a writer and thinker.

His first important work, *Oedipe,* won him immediate fame as well as a pension from the government. Aside from his artistic ability, he also functioned shrewdly as a business-man and managed to accumulate a sizable fortune while still in his twenties. During this time he gained several enemies, and in 1726 found himself again in the *Bastille* on trumped-up charges. He was released shortly thereafter on his promise that he would leave France. Thus, thoroughly disenchanted with the machinations of French justice, toward whose re-form he devoted himself for the rest of his life, he journeyed to England. He spent two years there, made many literary friends and came under the influence of the work of Newton and Locke.

He returned to France in 1729 and, deeply impressed with the comparative freedom of thought and expression that existed in England, quickly became a national figure through his own writings.

After a long correspondence with Frederick II, Emperor

of Prussia, Voltaire went to Berlin to take up residence at Frederick's court. He lived there until 1753 when, after a falling out with the Prussian ruler, he was forced to flee to Switzerland. In Geneva he solidified his position as a drama-tist of the first rank and continued to write in just about every area of human life, with special emphasis on history, science, law and religion. In 1759 he composed his most memorable work, *Candide,* a masterpiece of dramatic style and philosophical insight.

Undoubtedly the most active man of his era, Voltaire dipped his mind into practically every field of human expe-rience and became one of the most powerful men of all time. He died in Paris at the age of 84.

This volume, *The Philosophy of History,* was first pub-lished in London in 1766 and is a typical representation of Voltaire's attitude toward life and reality. His prime concern was to disprove and demolish the established notions that governed contemporary affairs but which were, in his pene-trating view, patently ridiculous. He spread this iconoclastic aim through all his work. The model for all subsequent dis-senters, he wrote with courage and conviction, and most important of all, with a controlled genius that lent to his words and ideas a strength and aggregate that has success-fully resisted the erosive influence of time.

THOMAS KIERNAN

CONTENTS

I

INTRODUCTION

YOU WISH that ancient history had been written by philosophers, because you are desirous of reading it as a philosopher. You seek for nothing but useful truths, and you say you have scarce found anything but useless errors. Let us endeavor mutually to enlighten one another; let us endeavor to dig some precious monuments from under the ruins of ages.

We will begin by examining, whether the globe, which we inhabit, was formerly the same as it is at present.

Perhaps our world has undergone as many changes, as its states have revolutions. It seems incontestable that the ocean formerly extended itself over immense tracts of land, now covered with great cities, and producing plenteous crops. You know that those deep shell-beds, which are found in Touraine and elsewhere, could have been gradually deposited only by the flowing of the tide, in a long succession of ages. Touraine, Britanny and Normandy, with their contiguous lands, were for a much longer time part of the ocean, than they have been provinces of France and Gaul.

Can the floating sands of the northern parts of Africa, and the banks of Syria in the vicinity of Egypt, be anything else but sands of the sea, remaining in heaps upon the gradual ebbing of the tide? Herodotus, who does not always lie,

1

doubtless relates a very great truth, when he says, that according to the relations given by the Egyptian priests, the Delta was not always land. May we not say the same of the sandy countries towards the Baltic sea? Do not the Cyclades manifestly indicate, by all the flats that surround them, by the vegetations, which are easily perceptible under the water that washes them, that they made part of the continent?

The Straights of Sicily, that ancient gulf of Charybdis and Scylla, still dangerous for small barks, do they not seem to tell us that Sicily was formerly joined to Apuleia, as the ancients always thought? Mount Vesuvius and mount Etna have the same foundations under the sea, which separates them. Vesuvius did not begin to be a dangerous volcano, till Etna ceased to be so; one of their mouths casts forth flames, when the other is quiet. A violent earthquake swallowed up that part of this mountain, which united Naples to Sicily.

All Europe knows that the sea overflowed one-half of Friesland. About forty years ago, I saw the church steeples of eighteen villages, near Mardyke, which still appeared above the inundation, but have since yielded to the force of the waves. It is reasonable to think that the sea in time quits its ancient banks. Observe Aiguemonte, Frejus, and Ravenna, which were all sea-ports, but are no longer such: Observe Damietta, where we landed in the time of the Crusades, and which is now actually ten miles distant from the shore, in the midst of land. The sea is daily retiring from Rosetta: nature every where testifies those revolutions; and if stars have been lost in the immensity of space, if the seventh Pleiade has long since disappeared, if others have vanished from sight into the milky way, should we be surprised that this little globe of ours undergoes perpetual changes?

I dare not, however, aver that the sea has formed or even washed all the mountains of the earth. The shells which have been found near mountains, may have there been left by some small testacious fish, the inhabitants of lakes; and these lakes, which have been moved by earthquakes, may have formed other lakes of inferior note. Ammon's horns, the starry stones, the lenticulars, the judaics, and glossopetrae appeared to me as terrestrial fossils. I did not dare think that these glossopetrae could be the tongues of sea dogs; and I am of opinion with him who said one might as easily believe that some thousands of women came and deposited their *conchae veneris* upon a shore, as to think that thousands of sea dogs came there to leave their tongues.

Let us take care not to mingle the dubious with the certain, the false with the true; we have proofs enough of the great revolutions of the globe, without going in search of fresh ones.

The greatest of these revolutions would be the loss of the Atlantic land, if it were true that this part of the world ever existed. It is probable that this land consisted of nothing else than the island of Madeira, discovered perhaps by the Phenicians, the most enterprising navigators of antiquity, forgotten afterwards, and at length rediscovered, in the beginning of the fifteenth century of our vulgar era.

In short, it evidently appears by the slopes of all the

3

lands which are washed by the ocean, by those gulfs which the eruptions of the sea have formed, by those archipelagoes that are scattered in the midst of the waters, that the two hemispheres have lost upwards of two thousand leagues of land on one side, which they have regained on the other.

II

OF THE DIFFERENT RACES OF MEN

WHAT IS the most interesting to us, is the sensible difference in the species of men, who inhabit the four known quarters of the world.

None but the blind can doubt that the whites, the negroes, the Albinoes, the Hottentots, the Laplanders, the Chinese, the Americans, are races entirely different.

No curious traveller ever passed through Leyden, without seeing part of the *reticulum mucosum* of a negro dissected by the celebrated Ruish. The remainder of this membrane is in the cabinet of curiosities at Petersburg. This membrane is black, and communicates to negroes that inherent blackness, which they do not lose, but in such disorders as may destroy this texture, and allow the grease to issue from its cells, and form white spots under the skin.

Their round eyes, squat noses, and invariable thick lips, the different configuration of their ears, their woolly heads, and the measure of their intellects, make a prodigious difference between them and other species of men; and what demonstrates, that they are not indebted for this difference to their climates, is that negro men and women, being transported into the coldest countries, constantly produce animals of their own species; and that mulattoes are only a bastard race of black men and white women, or white men and

5

black women, as asses, specifically different from horses, produce mules by copulating with mares.

The Albinoes are, indeed, a very small and scarce nation; they inhabit the center of Africa. Their weakness does not allow them to make excursions far from the caverns which they inhabit; the negroes, nevertheless, catch some of them at times, and these we purchase of them as curiosities. I have seen two of them, a thousand other Europeans have seen some. To say that they are dwarf negroes, whose skin has been blanched by a kind of leprosy, is like saying that the blacks themselves are whites blackened by the leprosy. An Albino no more resembles a Guinea negro, than he does an Englishman or a Spaniard. Their whiteness is not like ours, it does not appear like flesh, it has no mixture of white and brown; it is the color of linen, or rather of bleached wax; their hair and eye-brows are like the finest and softest silk; their eyes have no sort of similitude with those of other men, but they come very near partridge's eyes. Their shape resembles that of the Laplanders, but their head that of no other nation whatever; as their hair, their eyes, their ears, are all different, and they have nothing that seems to belong to man but the stature of their bodies, with the faculty of speaking and thinking, but in a degree very different from ours.

The apron, which nature has given to the Caffres, and whose flabby and lank skin falls from their navel half way down their thighs; the black breasts of the Samoiedes women, the beard of the males of our continent, and the beardless chins of the Americans, are such striking distinctions, that

6

it is scarce possible to imagine that they are not each of them of different races.

But now, if it should be asked, from whence came the Americans, it should be asked from whence came the inhabitants of the Terra Australis; and it has been already answered, that the same providence which placed men in Norway, planted some also in America and under the antarctic circle, in the same manner as it planted trees and made grass to grow there.

Several of the learned have surmised, that some races of men, or animals approximating to men, have perished: the Albinoes are so few in number, so weak, and so ill used by the negroes, that there is reason to apprehend this species will not long subsist.

Satyrs are mentioned by all the ancient writers. I do not see why their existence should be impossible: monsters brought forth by women are still stifled in Calabria. It is not improbable that in hot countries, monkeys may have enslaved girls. Herodotus in his second book, says, that in his Voyage into Egypt, there was a woman in the province of Mendes, who publicly copulated with a he-goat; and he calls all Egypt to witness the truth of it. It is forbidden in Leviticus, chapter seventeen to commit abominations with he and she-goats. These copulations must then have been common, and till such time as we are better informed, it is to be presumed that a monstrous species must have arisen from these abominable amours; but if such did exist, they could have no influence over the human kind; and like the mules, who do not engender, they could not interrupt the course of nature in the other races.

With respect to the duration of the life of man (if you abstract that line of Adam's descendants, consecrated by the Jewish books) it is probable that all the races of man have enjoyed a life nearly as short as our own; as animals, trees and all productions of nature, have ever had the same duration.

But it should be observed, that commerce not having always introduced among mankind the productions and disorders of other climates, and men being more robust and laborious in the simplicity of a country life, for which they are born, they must have enjoyed a more equal health, and a life somewhat longer than in effeminacy, or in the unhealthy works of great cities; that is to say, that if in Constantinople, Paris, or London, one man in 20,000 attains the age of an hundred years, it is probable that twenty men in twenty years arrived formerly at that age. This is seen in several parts of America, where mankind have preserved a pure state of nature.

The plague and the small pox, which the Arabian caravans communicated in a course of years to the people of Asia and Europe, were for a long time unknown. Thus mankind in Asia and the fine climates of Europe multiplied more easily than elsewhere. Accidental disorders, and some wounds were not, indeed, cured, as they are at present; but the advantage of never being afflicted with the plague or smallpox, compensated all the dangers attendant on our nature; so that, every thing considered, it is to be believed that human kind formerly enjoyed in the favorable climates a more healthy and happy life, than since the foundation of great empires.

III

OF THE ANTIQUITY OF NATIONS

ALMOST EVERY people, but particularly those of Asia, reckon a succession of ages, which terrifies us. This conformity among them should at least excite us to enquire, whether their ideas of antiquity were destitute of all probability.

It certainly requires a prodigious length of time for a nation to unite as one body of people, to become powerful, warlike, and learned. Look to America; there were but two kingdoms in that quarter of the globe when it was discovered; and the art of writing was not yet invented in either of those kingdoms. All the other parts of this vast continent were divided, and still are, into small societies to whom arts are unknown. All the colonies live in huts; they cover themselves with the skins of animals in the cold climates, and go almost naked in those that are temperate. The first live by hunting, the others upon kneaded roots. They have not fought after any other kind of life, because we never desire what we are unacquainted with. Their industry cannot extend beyond their pressing wants. The Samoiedes, the Laplanders, the inhabitants north of Siberia, and those of Kamchatka, have made still less progress than the people of America. The greatest part of the negroes and all the Caffres, are plunged in one same stupidity.

A concurrence of favorable circumstances for ages, are necessary to form a great society of men, united under the same laws. The like is necessary to form a language. Men would not articulate sounds, if they were not taught to pronounce words; they would utter nothing but a confused noise, and could not be understood but by signs. A child speaks after some time, only by imitation; and he would deliver himself with great difficulty, if he remained tongue-tied in his early years.

More time was perhaps necessary for men endowed with particular talents, to teach others the first rudiments of an imperfect and barbarous language, than was afterwards needful to compass the establishment of some society. There are some whole nations who have never been able to form a regular language and a distinct pronunciation. Such were even the Troglodites, according to Pliny. Such are still those who inhabit toward the Cape of Good Hope. But what a space still remains between this barbarous jargon, and the art of painting one's ideas! the distance is immense.

That state of brutes, in which human-kind remained a long time, must needs have rendered the species infinitely scarce in all climates. Men could hardly supply their wants, and not understanding each other, they could communicate no mutual assistance. Carnivorous beasts having a stronger instinct than they, must have covered the earth, and devoured part of the human species.

Man could not defend himself against ferocious animals, but by throwing stones, and arming himself with thick branches of trees; and from thence, perhaps, arose that con-

10

fused notion of antiquity, that the first heroes combated lions and wild boars with clubs.

The most populous countries were doubtless in hot climates, where man easily found a plentiful subsistence in cocoa, dates, pineapples and rice, which grows spontaneously. It is very probable that India, China, the banks of the Euphrates, and the Tigris, were very populous, when the other regions were almost desolate. On the other hand, in our northern climates, it was more easy to meet with a herd of wolves than a society of men.

IV

OF THE KNOWLEDGE OF THE SOUL

WHAT NOTION had the first people of the soul? The fame which all our boors have, before they have understood their catechism, or even after they understood it. They only acquire confused ideas, which they never reflect upon. Nature has been too kind to them to make them metaphysicians: that nature is perpetual, and every where alike. She made the first societies sensible that there was a being superior to man, when they were afflicted with uncommon misfortunes. She in the same manner taught them, that there is something in man which acts and thinks. They did not distinguish this faculty from that of life.

By what degrees can one arrive at imagining, in our physical being, another metaphysical being? Men, entirely occupied with their wants, were certainly not philosophers.

In the course of time societies somewhat polished were formed, in which a small number of men were at leisure to think. It must have happened that a man sensibly affected with the death of his father, his brother, or his wife, saw the person whose loss he regretted in his dream: two or three dreams of this sort must have caused uneasiness throughout a whole colony. Behold a dead corpse appearing to the living, and yet the deceased, remaining in the same place, with the worms gnawing him! This then, that wanders in the air, is something that was in him. It is his soul, his shade, his manes; it is a superficial figure of himself. Such is the natural reasoning of ignorance, which begins to reason. This is the opinion of all the primitive known times, and must consequently have been that of those unknown. The idea of a being purely immaterial could not have presented itself to the imagination of those who were acquainted with nothing but matter. Smiths, carpenters, masons, laborers, were necessary, before a man was found who had leisure to meditate. All manual arts, doubtless, preceded metaphysics for many ages.

We should remark, by the bye, that in the middle age of Greece, in the time of Homer, the soul was nothing more than an aerial image of the body. Ulysses saw shades and manes in hell; could he see spirits?

We shall, in the sequel, consider how the Greeks borrowed from the Egyptians the idea of hell and the apotheosis of the dead; how they believed, as well as other people, in a second life, without suspecting the spirituality of the soul: on the contrary, they could not imagine that an incorporeal being could be susceptible of either good or evil: and I do, not know whether Plato was not the first who spoke of a being purely spiritual. This, perhaps, is one of the greatest efforts of human knowledge. We are not, at this time of day, such novices upon that subject, and yet we consider the world as still unformed and scarcely fashioned.

V

OF THE RELIGION OF THE FIRST MEN

WHEN, AFTER a number of ages, several societies were formed, it is credible that there was some religion, a kind of rustic worship. Man, at that time entirely occupied with providing the necessaries of life, could not soar to the Author of life; he could not be acquainted with the connections of the various parts of the universe, those innumerable causes and effects, which to the wife proclaim an eternal architect.

The knowledge of a God, creator, requiter, and avenger, is the fruit of cultivated reason, or of revelation.

All people were therefore, for ages, what the inhabitants of the several coasts of Africa, of several islands, and half the Americans, are at present. Those people have no idea of a sole God, creator of all things, omnipresent, and exist' ing of himself to all eternity. They should not, however, be called atheists in the usual sense; for they do not deny a supreme being; they are not acquainted with him; they have no idea of him. The Caffres take an insect for their protector, the negroes a serpent. Among the Americans, some adore the moon, others a tree. Several have no worship whatever.

The Peruvians, when they became polished, adored the fun. Either Mango Capac had made them believe that he was the son of that planet, or a dawn of reason made them

14

think they owed some acknowledgment to the planet which animated nature.

In order to know how these different doctrines and superstitions gained ground, it seems to me necessary to follow the career of human understanding left alone without a guide. The inhabitants of a village, who are little better than savages, perceive the fruits which should nourish them perish: an inundation carries away some cabins: others are destroyed by thunder. Who has done them this mischief? It could not be one of their fellow citizens, for they have all equally suffered. It is therefore some secret power that has afflicted them, and must therefore be appeased. How is it to be effected? by using it as they do those whom they are desirous of pleasing; in making it some small presents. There is a serpent in the neighborhood; it is very likely the serpent: they offer him milk near the cavern, whither he retires; from that time he becomes sacred: he is invoked when they are at war with the neighboring village, who, on their side, have chosen another protector.

Other little colonies find themselves in the same situation. But there being no object near them to excite their terror and adoration, they call in general the being whom they suspect has done them mischief, the master, the lord, the chief, the ruler.

This idea being more conformable than the others to the dawn of reason, which increases and strengthens with time, possesses every one's head, when the nation is become more numerous. Thus we find that many nations have had no other god than their master, their lord. Such was Adonai among the Phenicians, Baal, Milkom, and Adad, with the

15

people of Syria. All these names signify nothing more than the Lord, the Powerful.

Every state, then, had in time its tutelar divinity, without knowing even what was a god, or being able to imagine that the neighboring state was not equally furnished as themselves, with a real protector. For how could they think, when they had a lord, that others had not one also? The only thing to be known was, which among so many matters, lords, and gods, would be victorious, when the nations fought against each other.

This was doubtless the origin of that opinion, which so generally and so long prevailed, that every people was really protected by the divinity they had chosen. This idea was so deeply rooted in men, that in after-times, it was adopted by the Jews themselves. Jephtha said to the Ammonites, "Do you not possess by right, what your lord Chamos has given you? suffer us, then, to possess the land which our lord Adonai has promised unto us."

There are two other passages equally strong, which are those of Jeremiah and Isaiah, where it is said, "what reason had the lord Melkom to take possession of the land of Gad?" It is evident by these expressions, that the Jews, though servants to Adonai, acknowledged, nevertheless, the lord Melkom and the lord Chamos.

Still farther: nothing was more common than to adopt strange gods. The Greeks acknowledged those of the Egyptians; I do not mean Apis's bull and Anubis's dog, but Ammon and the twelve great gods. The Romans adored all the gods of the Greeks. Jeremiah, Amos, and St. Stephen, assure us, that the Jews for forty years in the desert acknowledged

16

no other than Moloc, Remphan, and Kicim; that they made no sacrifice, and presented no offering to the lord Adonai, whom they afterwards adored. It is true that the Pentateuch speaks of nothing but the golden calf, which no prophet mentions: but this is not the place to clear up this great difficulty; it is sufficient that they equally revered Moses, Jeremiah, Amos, and St. Stephen, who seem to contradict one another, and yet are reconciled.

I shall observe only, that, except in time of war and bloody fanaticism, which extinguished all humanity, and which rendered the manners, laws, and religion of a people, the objects of horror to another people, all nations were very well satisfied that their neighbors had their own particular gods; and that they frequently imitated the worship and ceremonies of strangers.

The Jews themselves, though they looked with horror upon the rest of men, which detestation increased with time, imitated the circumcision of the Arabs and Egyptians; like the last they accustomed themselves to make a distinction of meats; borrowed from them ablutions, processions, and sacred dances, the hazel goat, and red cow. They often adored the Baal and Belphigor of their neighbors; so much do nature and custom prevail over law, particularly when that law is not generally known to the people. Thus Jacob, grandson to Abraham, made no difficulty of wedding two sisters, who were what we call idolaters, and daughters to an idolatrous father. Moses himself espoused the daughter of an idolatrous Midianite.

Those same Jews, who made such an outcry against strange worships, called, in their sacred books, Nabuchodo-

17

nosor, the anointed of the lord; and the idolater Cyrus, also the anointed of the lord. One of their prophets was sent to the idolater Ninevus. Elisha allowed the idolater Naaman to go into the temple of Remnan. But to avoid anticipation; we know well enough that men constantly run-counter to the laws by their manners. Let us not lose sight of the subject we were considering, but continue to observe how different religions were established.

The most polished people of Asia, on this side the Euphrates, adored the planets. The Chaldeans, before the time of Zoroaster, paid homage to the sun; as did afterwards the Peruvians in another hemisphere. This error must be very natural to man, as it has had so many followers in Asia and America. A small and half savage nation has but one protector. Does it become more numerous? the number of its gods is increased. The Egyptians began by adoring Isheth or Iris, and they at last adored cats. The first homage the rustic Romans paid was to Mars; that of the Romans, masters of Europe, was to the goddess of marriage and the god of thieves. Nevertheless, Cicero, all the philosophers, and those initiated, acknowledge a supreme and omnipotent God. They were all brought back to that point of reason, from whence savage men had departed by instinct.

The apotheosis could not have been devised till long after the first kinds of worship. It is not natural immediately to make a god of a man whom we saw born like ourselves, suffer like us maladies, chagrin, the miseries of humanity, subject to the same humiliating wants, die and become food for worms. But this is what happened to almost all nations, after the revolutions of several ages.

A man who had done great things, who had been service-able to human nature, could not in truth be looked upon as a god, by those who had seen him tremble with the ague, and seek for clothing: but enthusiasts persuade themselves that, being possessed of eminent qualities, he had them from a god. In the same manner gods produced children all over the world; for without enumerating the dreams of so many people who preceded the Greeks, Bacchus, Perseus, Hercules, Castor, and Pollux, were sons of Gods. Romulus was a son of God, Alexander was proclaimed a son of God in Egypt; one Odin, with us northern nations, was a son of God; Mango Capac was son of the sun in Peru. The historian of the Moguls, Abulgazi, relates that one of the grandmothers of Gingiskan, named Alanku, when a girl, was impregnated by a celestial ray. Gingiskan himself passed for the son of God. And when Pope Innocent sent brother Asulin to Ba-toukan, grandson to Genghis, this monk, who could not be presented but to one of the viziers, said he came from the vicar of God; the minister replied, is this vicar ignorant that he should pay homage and tribute to the son of God, the great Batoukan his master?

With men fond of the marvelous, there is no great distance between a son of God and God. After two or three generations, the son partakes of the father's dominion. Thus temples were raised to all those who were supposed to be born from the supernatural correspondence of the divinity with our wives and daughters.

Volumes might be written upon this subject; but all these volumes might be reduced to two words, which are that the majority of mankind were for a long time in a state of insensibility and imbecility, and that, perhaps, the most insensible of all were those who wanted to discover a signifi-cation in those absurd fables, and ingraft reason upon folly.

VI

OF THE CUSTOMS AND OPINIONS OF ALL THE ANCIENT NATIONS

NATURE BEING every where the same, men must nec´ essarily have adopted the same truths, and fallen into the same errors, in regard to those things which are the imme´ diate objects of sense, and the most striking to the imagina´ tion. They must have attributed the noise and effects of thunder to some superior being inhabiting the air. The people bordering upon the ocean, seeing great tides inundate their coasts at the time of full moon, must naturally have imputed to the moon, the various effects which attended her different phases.

Among animals, the serpent must have appeared to them endowed with superior intelligence; because seeing it some´ times cast its skin, they had reason to think it became young again. It might, then, by repeating this change, always remain youthful, and it was therefore believed immortal: so was it in Egypt and Greece the symbol of immortality. The larger serpents which were found near fountains, terrified the timo´ rous from approaching them; and hence they were soon imag´ ined to be the guardians of hidden treasures. Thus a serpent was the fabled guard of the golden apples of the Hesperides; another watched over the golden fleece; and in celebrating

21

the mysteries of Bacchus, the image of a serpent was carried, which seemed to guard a golden grape.

The serpent thus passing for the most subtle of animals, hence arose that ancient Indian fable, that God having created man, gave him a drug, which insured him a healthful and long life; but that man entrusted this divine present with his ass, who, upon the road, becoming thirsty, was seduced to a neighboring fountain by a serpent, who pretended to hold his burden while he was drinking: thus it was that man by his negligence lost immortality, and the serpent gained it by his subtlety. Hence innumerable tales of asses and serpents.

Serpents were found, indeed, to be mischievous animals; but as they were supposed to possess something divine, nothing less than a deity was imagined capable of destroying them. Thus the serpent Python was killed by Apollo, and the great serpent Ophioneus waged far for a length of time against the gods, before the Greeks had framed their Apollo. We find it related in a fragment of Phericides, that this fable of the great serpent, the enemy to the gods, was one of the most ancient among the Phenicians.

We have already found that dreams must have introduced the same superstition all over the earth. If whilst awake, I am uneasy for my wife or son's health, and in my sleep I see them in the agonies of death; should they die a few days after, it is not to be doubted that the gods sent me this warning. Is my dream not accomplished? it was a fallacious representation, which the gods were pleased to terrify me with. Thus in Homer, Jupiter sends a fallacious dream to Agamemnon, chief of the Greeks. Indeed all dreams, true or false, the superstitious supposed to come from heaven. In the like manner oracles were supposed to be ordained upon earth.

Does a woman apply to the magi to know whether her husband will die within the year or not? one of them answers yes, the other no. It is certain that one of them must be in the right; if her husband lives, she says nothing of the matter; if he dies, she proclaims all over the city that the magi, who foretold his death, was a divine prophet. There are men in all countries who prognosticate events, and who discover the most latent things. With the Egyptians these men were called the seers, as Manethian relates after Joseph, in his discourse against Appion.

There were seers in Chaldea and Syria. Every temple had its oracles; those of Apollo gained such great credit, that Rollin, in his Ancient History, records the oraculous predictions of Apollo to Croesus. The god divines that the king will dress a tortoise in a brass pan; and replies to the question Croesus puts to him concerning the length of his reign, that it will end when a mule mounts the throne of the Persians. Rollin does not enquire whether these predictions, worthy only of Nostradamus, were not made after the predicted event had happened. He does not in the least question the foreknowledge of the priests of Apollo, but believes that God allowed Apollo to speak truth. This probably was to confirm the Pagans in their religion.

The origin of good and evil is a more philosophical question, which all the great polished nations have agreed on, from Judea to Greece.

The first theologues of all nations must have put the

23

same question which we do from the age of fifteen, Why is there any evil upon earth?

It was taught in India, that Adimo, the daughter of Brama, brought forth from her navel, the just from her right side and the unjust from her left; and that it was from this left side that we originally deduced physical and moral evil. The Egyptians had their Typhon, who was the enemy of Osiris. The Persians imagined that Arimanes pierced the egg, which Aromase laid, and communicated to it sin. We know the Pandora of the Greeks: this is the finest of all the allegories which antiquity has handed down to us.

The allegory of Job was certainly wrote in Arabic, as the Hebrew and Greek versions have retained several Arabic terms. This book, which is of great antiquity, represents Satan, who is the Arimanes of the Persians, and the Typhon of the Egyptians, as wandering over the earth and asking permission of the lord to afflict Job. Satan seems indeed to be in subordination to the lord; but it afterwards appears that Satan is a very powerful being, capable of inflicting disorders, and destroying the animal world.

So many people really agreed, without knowing it, in the belief of two principles, that so much of the universe as was then known was in some measure Manichean.

Every people must have allowed expiations, for where was the man who had not been guilty of great injuries against society? and where was the man whose natural in-stinct did not prompt him to remorse? Water cleansed their body and vestments of filth, fire purified metals; it was there-fore necessary that water and fire should purify souls: nor were there any temples without holy water and sacred fire.

Men plunged themselves into the Ganges, into the Indus, and into the Euphrates, when it was new moon, and particularly during the eclipses. This immersion expiated their sins. If they did not purify themselves in the Nile, it was only for fear that the penitents might have been devoured by crocodiles. But the priests who purified themselves for the people, plunged themselves into large tubs of water, where they also bathed those criminals who came to ask pardon of the gods.

The Greeks had in all their temples sacred baths, as well as sacred fires, which were universal symbols with all men of the purity of souls. In a word, superstition seems to have been established in all nations and among all people, except the men of letters in China.

VII

OF SAVAGES

DO YOU understand by savages, those rustics who live in cabins with their females, and some animals, incessantly exposed to all the intemperance of the seasons, acquainted with nothing but the earth that nourishes them; the market where they sometimes repair to sell their commodities, in order to purchase some coarse raiments; speaking a jargon which is unintelligible in cities; furnished with few ideas, and consequently few expressions; subjected, without knowing why, to a penman, to whom they carry every year half of what they have earned by the sweat of their brow; meeting upon certain days in a kind of barn, to celebrate ceremonies which they no way comprehend; listening to a man dressed differently from themselves, whom they do not in the least understand; sometimes quitting their cottages at the beat of a drum, and engaging to go and fight in foreign lands, to slay their own likenesses, for a quarter of what they would earn by working at home? There are such savages as these all over Europe. It must certainly be agreed that the people of Canada, and the Caffres, whom we have been pleased to style savages, are infinitely superior to our own. The Huron, the Algonquin, the Illinois, the Caffre, the Hottentot, have the art of fabricating every thing that is needful for them; this art our rustics are wanting in. The colonies

26

of America and Africa are free, and our savages have not even the idea of freedom.

The supposed savages of America receive ambassadors from our colonies, which avarice and imprudence have transplanted near their territories. They are acquainted with honor, which none of our European savages ever heard mentioned. They have a country, they love it and defend it; they make treaties, they fight courageously, and often speak with heroic energy. Is there a finer reply from all Plutarch's great men than that of the chief of the Canadians, to whom a European nation proposed ceding their patrimony: "We were born upon this land, our fathers were buried here, can we say to our fathers bones, Rise up and come with us into a foreign land?"

These Canadians are Spartans, in comparison to our rustics, who vegetate in our villages, and the Sybarites, who enervate themselves in our cities.

Do you understand by savages two-footed animals, walking occasionally upon their hands, wandering alone in forests, *salvatici, selvagi,* copulating at a venture, forgetting the females to whom they were united, equally unacquainted with their fathers and their children, driving like brutes, without the instinct and resources of brutes? Writers have averred this to be the true state of man, and that we have only miserably degenerated, since we have changed. I do not think this solitary life, which our forefathers are supposed to have led, is in human nature.

We are, if I mistake not, in the foremost rank (if it is allowable to be said) of animals living in herds, like bees, ants, beavers, geese, fowls, sheep, etc. If we meet with a straggling bee, is it to be concluded that it is in a state of pure nature, and that those who work in the hive are de-generated?

Has not every animal his peculiar instinct, which he is necessarily compelled to obey? what is this instinct? the dis-position of the organs, the motion of which time discovers. This instinct cannot display itself immediately, because the organs have not acquired their greatest perfection.

> Leur pouvoir est constant, leur principe est divin,
> Il faut que l'enfant croisse avant qu'il les exerce;
> Il ne les connait pas sous la main qui le berce,
> Le moineau dans l'instant qu'il a reçû le jour,
> Sans plumes dans son nid peut-il sentir l'amour?
> Le renard en naissant va-t-il chercher sa proye?
> Les insectes changeants qui nous filent la soye,
> Les essains bourdonnants de ces filles du ciel,
> Qui pétrissent la cire, & composent le miel,
> Si-tôt qu'ils sont éclos forment-ils leur ouvrage?
> Tout s'accroit par le temps, tout meurit avec l'âge.
> Chaque être a son objet, & dans l'instant marqué
> Marche & touche à son but par le ciel indiqué.

> Their principles a sacred instinct moves,
> And truth's unvaried law their power improves:
> But these th' unconscious infant cannot feel,
> 'Til strength and ripen'd thought such powers reveal.
> Can the young fibres of the unfeather'd dove
> So soon confess the soft alarms of love?
> Or dare the new-faln fox through forests rove?
> The changling worm that spins the silken clue,
> The bee who sips the flower's ambrosial dew,
> Whose wondrous art and industry might vie
> With the fair sisters of the peopled sky;
> Do they first springing from their parent soil,

28

While yet untaught, attempt their curious toil?
Not so! all nature's children grow with time,
Age ripens every fruit in every clime.
Each being here endu'd with fittest power
Has still its object at the appointed hour:
Improv'd by strength and gradually refin'd,
Moves and attains the goal by heaven design'd.

Do we not really see that all animals, as well as every other being, invariably execute that law which nature has prescribed to their species? The bird builds its nest, as the stars perform their course, by a principle which can never alter. Why should man only have changed? had he been destined to pursue a solitary life, like the other carnivorous animals, could he so far counteract the law of nature as to live in society? and if he were made to live in herds like animals of the barton, could he immediately have perverted his destiny to that degree, as to live for ages in solitude? He is in a state of amelioration, and from thence it is concluded that his nature has been perverted; but why may it not be inferred that he has arrived at that degree of perfection which nature has limited to humanity?

All mankind live in society; can we from thence deduce that they were not in the same state formerly? Would this not be like concluding that bulls were not formerly possessed of horns, because they do not now exist without them?

Men in general have ever been what they now are: by this I would not mean to say that they always had fine cities, cannon that were twenty-four-pounders, comic operas, and religious convents; but man always had the same instinct, which prompted him to love himself, in the companion of his

29

pleasures, in his children, in his grandchildren, in the works of his hands.

This is immutable all over the universe. The foundation of society ever existing, there has therefore ever been some society, and we were consequently not made to live like bears.

Strayed children have sometimes been found in woods, living like brutes; but sheep and geese have also been found in the same state. This does not disprove that geese and sheep were destined to live in herds. Some Faquirs in India live all alone loaded with chains. Even so, and they live in this manner that passengers may admire them, and bestow alms upon them. They perform through a kind of vain fanaticism, what our beggars do, who lame themselves to excite compassion. These excrements of human society are only proofs how far that society may be abused.

It is very probable that men were in a state of rusticity for many thousand ages, as an infinite number of peasants are to this very hour. But men could not live like badgers and hares.

By what law, by what secret ties, by what instinct, could men always have lived like a family, without the assistance of art, and without having yet formed a language? It must have been by their own nature, by the taste, which prompts them to an union with females; by the attachment which an Icelander, a Laplander, or a Hottentot, feels for his mate, when the protuberance of her belly gives him hope of seeing born of his blood a being like himself; by the reciprocal aid which this man and this woman furnish each other; by the love which nature inspires them with for the little one as soon as he is born; by the habitual love they have for him;

by the habitual obedience which the child necessarily pays to his father and mother; by the assistance which he gives them when he has attained his fifth or sixth year; by the successive children they produce; in a word, because they see with pleasure, in an advanced age, their sons and daughters produce other children, who have the same instinct as their fathers and mothers.

I acknowledge this is a very unpolished society of men: but is it believed that the colliers in the forests of Germany, the inhabitants of the North, and a hundred different people of Africa, live at this very time in a manner that is extremely different?

What language will these savage and barbarous families speak? they will, doubtless, be for a long time without speaking: they will understand each other very well by sounds and gestures. All nations have thus been savages, taking the word in this sense; that is to say, there must have been, for a great length of time, wandering families in forests, disputing their food with other animals, arming themselves against them with stones and thick branches, feeding upon wild roots, fruits of various kinds, and at length even upon animals.

There is a mechanical instinct in man, which we see every day produces great effects in men of very confined intellects. We see machines invented by the inhabitants of the mountains of Tyrol and the Vosges, which astonish the learned. The most ignorant peasant knows how to raise the heaviest burdens by the assistance of the lever, not doubting that equilibrium power is in the weight, as the distance from the point of support to the weight, is at the same distance from this point of support to the power. If it had been necessary that this knowledge should have preceded the use of levers, what a number of ages would have elapsed before a large stone could have been moved from its place!

Let it be proposed to any children to jump over a ditch, they will all mechanically take their spring, by retiring a little backward, in order to have a run. They are certainly ignorant that their strength is in this case the product of their mass being multiplied by their swiftness.

It is then evinced that nature only inspires us with useful ideas, which precede all our reflexion. It is the same in morality. We are all possessed of two sentiments, which form the basis of society, pity and justice. If a child should see his likeness torn to pieces, he would be seized by sudden agonies, which he would testify by his cries and tears; and he would, if it were in his power, succor the sufferer.

Ask a child who has had no education, who begins to speak and reason, if the grain which a man has sown in his field belongs to him, and if the robber who has slain its proprietor, has a legal right to that grain: you will find whether the child does not reply in the same manner as would all the legislators of the earth.

God has implanted in us a principle of reason that is universal, as he has given feathers to birds and skins to bears: and this principle is so immutable, that it subsists in despite of all the passions which oppose it, in despite of those tyrants who would drown it in blood, in despite of those impostors who would annihilate it by superstition. It is for this reason, that the most unpolished people constantly judge very well in the end of those laws by which they are governed, because they are sensible whether those laws are agreeable or op-

32

posite to the principles of pity and justice, which are implanted in their hearts.

But before a numerous society, a people, or a nation,
can be formed, it is necessary that some language should be
established, this is the greatest difficulty to be surmounted.
Without the gift of imitation, it would never have been
overcome, they must doubtless have begun by sounds, which
must have expressed their first wants; afterwards the most
ingenious man, born with the most flexible organs, must
have formed some articulations, which their children repeated, and their mothers must have particularly untied
their tongues. Idioms in their first state must have consisted
of monosyllables, being the most easy to form and retain.

We really find that the most ancient nations, who have
preserved any thing of their primitive tongue, still express,
by monosyllables, the most familiar things which most immediately strike the senses: Chinese to this very hour is founded
upon monosyllables.

Consult the ancient Tudesc, and all the northern idioms,
you will scarce find any useful thing in common, expressed
by more than one articulation. It is all monosyllables; *zon*
the sun, *moun* the moon, *zé* the sea, *flus* a flood, *man* man,
hof the head, *boum* a tree, *drink* drink, *march* march, *shlaf*
sleep, etc.

This brevity of expression was used in the forests of Gaul
and Germany and all the north. The Greeks and Romans
had no words more compound, till a long time after they
were united as a body of people.

But what wisdom was necessary to distinguish the different senses? How came we to express the different grada-

33

tions *I would, I should have willed,* the positive things and those that are conditional? It could only have happened among those nations that were already most polished, that by dint of time they expressed with compound words, those secret operations of the human mind; so we find among the Barbarians there are but two or three tenses: the Hebrews made use of only the present and future tenses. And after all, notwithstanding all the efforts of man, no language comes near to perfection.

VIII

OF AMERICA

CAN IT still be asked from whence came the men who peopled America? The same question might be asked with regard to the Terra Australis. They are much farther distant from the port which Columbus set out from, than the Antilles. Men and beasts have been found in all parts of the earth that are inhabitable; Who placed them there? We have already answered he that caused the grass to grow in the fields; and it is no more surprising to find men in America, than it is to find flies there.

It is pleasant enough to read the Jesuit Lafiteau in his preface to the *History of the American Savages,* where he says, that none but atheists can pretend to say that God created the Americans.

Maps of the ancient world are still engraven, where America appears under the title of the Atlantic Island. The Cape Verde islands are there called the Gorgades, and the Caribbees the Hesperides. This is only founded upon the discovery of the Canary Islands, and probably that of Madeira, whither the Phenicians and the Carthaginians sailed; they are almost close to Africa, and, perhaps, they were not so far distant from it formerly as they are at present.

Let Father Lafiteau make the inhabitants of the Caribbees descend from Caria, by reason of the affinity of the name, and because the women of both served their husbands for cooks; let him imagine that Caribbeans produce red children, and negro women black, because their forefathers accustomed themselves to paint their skins black or red.

It happened, says he, that the negro women observing their husbands' complexions painted black, their imaginations were so much struck therewith, that their race ever after felt the effects of it. The same thing happened to the Caribbean women, who by the same strength of imagination brought forth red children. He supports his argument with the example of Jacob's lambs, who were born with spotted skins, by the art of that patriarch, who put in their view branches of trees half peeled; these branches appearing at some distance of two different colors, communicated their color to the lambs of this patriarch. But the Jesuit should know that what happened in the time of Jacob does not happen now.

If Laban's kinsman had been asked why his flocks, constantly seeing grass, did not produce green herds, he would have been somewhat embarrassed what to reply.

Lafiteau at length makes the Americans descend from the ancient Greeks, for which opinion he assigns the following reasons. The Greeks had their fables, the Americans have also fables; the first Greeks went a-hunting, the Americans also hunt; the first Greeks had oracles, the Americans have their sorcerers; there were dances performed at the feasts of the Greeks, the Americans dance. It must be allowed that these are very convincing reasons.

A reflection might be made upon the nations of the new world, which father Lafiteau has omitted, which is, that the people distant from the tropics have always been invincible; and that those people who were nearest the tropics have almost always been subdued by monarchs. It was for a long time the same in our continent; but we do not find that the people of Canada have ever attempted to subjugate Mexico, in the manner that the Tartars spread themselves over Asia and Europe. It should seem that the Canadians were never sufficiently numerous to detach colonies into other parts.

America in general could never have been so much peopled as Europe and Asia; it is covered with vast marshes, which render the air very unhealthy. Innumerable poisons are the produce of the earth; arrows steeped in the juice of these venomous herbs, always occasion mortal wounds. Nature, in fine, had given the Americans much less industry than the inhabitants of the ancient world: these causes united may have been greatly prejudicial to population.

Among the various physical observations which may be made upon this fourth part of our universe so long unknown, the most remarkable, perhaps, is that there is but one people who have any beards: these are the Esquimaux; they are situated about the fifty-second degree of northern latitude, where the cold is more intense than in sixty-six degrees of our continent; their neighbors are all beardless. Here then are two races of men absolutely different, bordering upon each other.

Towards the Isthmus of Panama is the race of the Dariens almost similar to the Albinoes, who shun light, and vegetate in caverns, a feeble race, and consequently not numerous.

The American lions are small and fearful; the sheep are

37

large, and so vigorous that they are used to carry burdens. All the lakes are at least ten times as large as ours; in a word, the natural productions of the earth are not like those of our hemisphere. Thus are all things variegated, and that same providence which produced the elephant, the rhinoceros, and negroes, has given birth in other regions to misfits, contours, swine with navels upon their backs, and men with dispositions quite different from ours.

IX

OF THE THEOCRACY

IT SEEMS that the greater part of the ancient nations were governed by a kind of theocracy. To begin by India, you there find the Bramans have long been sovereigns: in Persia the Magi have the greatest authority. The story of Smerdis's ears may very probably be a fable; but it will always follow that he was a magi upon the throne of Cyrus. Several Egyptian priests had so great a dominion over their kings, that they went so far as to prescribe to them how much they should eat and drink, brought up their children, tried them after their death, and often made themselves kings.

If we come down to the Greeks, however fabulous their history may be, do we not learn therefrom that the prophet Calcas had sufficient power in the army to sacrifice the daughter of the king of kings? Come still lower to the savage nations since the Greeks, the Druids governed the Gauls.

It does not seem to have been possible that in the first colonies, there could have been any other than a theocratic government; for as soon as a nation has chosen a tutelar god, this god has priests; these priests reign over the minds of the people, they cannot govern but in the name of God: they therefore always make him speak; they retail his oracles, and it is by an express order from God, that every thing is performed.

Hence the sacrifices of human blood, which have drenched almost all the earth. What father, what mother, would ever have abjured nature to that degree as to present their son or daughter to a priest, in order to be slain upon an altar, if they had not been certain that the god of their country had commanded the sacrifice.

Theocracy did not only reign for a long time, but it extended tyranny to the most shocking excess that human falsehood can prevail; and the more this government was called divine, the more it became abominable.

Almost every people have sacrificed their children to their gods; they therefore believed they received this unnatural mandate from the lips of those gods whom they adored.

Among the people who are so improperly called civilized, I see scarce any but the Chinese who have not been guilty of these shocking absurdities. China is the only one of all the ancient states which has not been under sacerdotal subjection. As to the Japanese they submitted to the laws imposed upon them by a priest, six hundred years before we were in being. Almost everywhere theocracy is so much established, so deeply rooted, that the first histories are those of gods themselves, who became incarnated to come and govern men. The gods, said the people of Thebes and Memphis, have reigned twelve thousand years in Egypt. Brama incarnated himself to reign in India, Samonocodom at Siam, the god Adad governed Syria, the goddess Cybele had been sovereign of Phrygia, Jupiter of Crete, Saturn of Greece and Italy. The same spirit runs through all these fables; it consists in a confused idea which men had, that the gods formerly descended upon earth.

40

X

OF THE CHALDEANS

THE MOST ancient polished nations appear to me to have been the Chaldeans, the Indians, and the Chinese. We have a certain epocha of the science of the Chaldeans: it was in the year 1903 of celestial observations sent from Babylon by Callistanus to the preceptor of Alexander. These astronomical tables form an exact retrospect to the year 2234, before our vulgar era. It is true that this epoch borders upon the time, when according to the Vulgate, the deluge took place. But let us not enter here into the depths of the different chronologies of the Vulgate, the Samaritan, and the Septuagint, which we equally revere. The universal deluge is a great miracle, which has no connection with our inquiries. We are reasoning here only according to natural opinions, constantly submitting the weak feelings of our shallow understandings to the enlightenings of a superior order.

Ancient authors, quoted by George Le Sincelle, say that in the time of a Chaldean king named Xixoutron, there happened a dreadful inundation. The Tigris and the Euphrates overflowed their banks, probably more than usual. But the Chaldeans could not have known otherwise than by revelation, that such a scourge had submerged all the habitable world. Once more let it be observed, I consider here only the usual course of nature.

41

It is certain that the Chaldeans had not existed upon earth more than 1900 years before our era: this short space would not have been sufficient for them to discover the true system of our universe; an amazing thought, which however, the Chaldeans at length compassed. Aristadreus of Samos, tells us that the sages of Chaldea were acquainted with the impossibility of the earth's occupying the center of the planetary world, and that they had assigned the sun this station, which belonged to him; that they made the earth, and other planets revolve round him, each in a different orb.

The progress of the mind is so slow, the illusion of our eyes so powerful, the submission to received ideas so tyrannical, that it is not possible for a people who had existed only nineteen hundred years to have arrived at that summit of philosophy, which contradicts the sight, and which requires the most profound theory. So did the Chaldeans reckon 470,000 years. Again, this knowledge of the true system of the world, was not the lot but of a small number of philosophers. This is the fate of all great truths; and the Greeks, who came afterwards, adopted nothing but the common system, which is the system of children.

Four hundred and seventy thousand years* are found im-

* Our holy religion, so superior in every thing to our understanding, teaches us that the world has been created only about six thousand years, according to the Septuagint. The interpreter of this ineffable religion teaches us that Adam had intuitive knowledge, and that all the arts were transmitted from Adam to Noah. If this is really the opinion of the church, we will adopt it with a firm and invariable faith, submitting, moreover, all we write to the judgment of that holy church, which is infallible. It is in vain that the emperor Julian, otherwise so respectable for his virtue, valor, and knowledge, says in his discourse, censured by the great and moderate St. Cirille, that whether Adam had intuitive knowledge or not, God could not have forbid him to touch the tree of knowledge of right and wrong; that God, on the

42

mense to us, who were born only yesterday; but this is a very little time for the whole universe. I know that we cannot adopt this reckoning, that Cicero made a joke of it, that it is extravagant, and moreover that we should rather give credit to the Pentateuch, than to Sanchoniaton or Berosus: but once more, it is impossible (humanly speaking) that men should in nineteen hundred years arrive at the knowledge of such astonishing truths. The first of all arts is that of providing sustenance, which formerly was more difficult for men than brutes; the second, to form a language, which certainly requires a very considerable space of time; the third, to build some huts; the fourth, to provide clothing. Then the forging of iron, or the supplying the want of it; these require so many lucky incidents, so much industry, so many ages, that it is surprising how men could any way compass them. What a leap from this state to astronomy!

The Chaldeans for a long time engraved their observations and their laws upon bricks in hieroglyphics: these were speaking characters, a custom which the Egyptians acquired after several ages had elapsed. The art of transmitting ideas by alphabetical characters, could not have been invented but very late in that part of Asia.

It may be supposed that when the Chaldeans built cities, they began to make use of the alphabet. How did they do before? Will it be answered, as we do in our village, and

contrary, should have commanded him to eat much of the fruit of this tree, in order to improve his intuitive knowledge, if he was possessed of it, or to acquire it, if he had it not. In a word, we constantly warn the reader, that we do not interfere in any respect with holy things. We protect against all erroneous interpretations, against all malicious inferences that may be adduced from our words.

43

in twenty thousand other villages of the world, where no one can either write or read, and where, nevertheless, people understand each other very well, where all the necessary arts are cultivated, and even sometimes with genius?

Babylon was probably a very ancient hamlet, before it was formed into an immense and superb city. But who built this city? was it Semiramis? was it Belus? was it Nabonassar? There never was in Asia any woman called Semiramis, nor any man called Belus. It is like our giving to Greek cities the names of Armagnac and, Abbeville. The Greeks, who changed all the barbarous terminations into Greek words, transmogrified all the Asiatic names. Moreover, the history of Semiramis resembles in all respects an oriental tale.

Nabonassar, or rather Nabon-assor, was probably the person who embellished and fortified Babylon, and at length rendered it so superb a city. He was a real monarch, known in Asia by the era which bears his name. This incontestable era did not begin till 1747 years before our own; so that it is very modern, when compared to the number of ages necessary to have established great dominions. It appears even by the name of Babylon, that it existed long before Nabonassar. It was the city of father Bel. Bab in Chaldean signifies father, as Herbelot acknowledges; Bel is the name of the Lord. The Orientals never knew it by any other name than Babel, the city of the Lord, the city of God, or according to others the door of God.

Neither was there such a person as Ninus the founder of Ninvah, which we call Nineveh, any more than Belus the founder of Babylon. Never did the name of any Asiatic prince terminate in *us*.

44

The circumference of Babylon might have been twenty-four of our middling leagues; but that one Ninus should have erected upon the Tyger at the distance of only forty leagues from Babylon, a city named Nineveh, of so great an extent, is what does not seem credible. Three powerful empires are said to have existed at the same time; namely, that of Babylon, that of Assyria or Nineveh, and that of Syria or Damascus: this has very little the air of probability; it is like saying that there were at the same time in a part of Gaul three powerful empires, the capitals of which were Paris, Soissons, and Orleans, each being twenty-four leagues in circumference. Besides, Nineveh was not built, or at least was of very little importance at the time when it is said that the prophet Jonas was appointed to exhort the people to perform penance, and was swallowed up in his way by a fish, which kept him in his belly three nights and three days.

The imaginary empire of Assyria was not yet in existence at the time that Jonas is introduced; for he prophesied, it is said, under the Melk or Jewish viceroy Joas; and Phul, who is looked upon in the Hebrew books as the first king of Assyria, did not reign, according to them, till about fifty-two years after the death of Joas. By confronting the dates in this manner, contradictions are every where discovered, and uncertainty necessarily follows.

I acknowledge I do not comprehend anything about the two empires of Babylon and Assyria. Several sages, who were desirous of throwing some light upon these obscurities, have affirmed that Assyria and Chaldea were one and the same empire, sometimes governed by two princes, one residing at Babylon, the other at Nineveh; and this reasonable opinion may be adopted, till such time as we discover one still more reasonable.

What contributes to give great probability to the antiq' uity of this nation, is that famous tower erected to observe the planetary world. Almost all the commentators, unable to dispute the existence of this monument, think themselves obliged to suppose that it was the remains of the tower of Babel, which men wanted to erect unto heaven. What the commentators mean by heaven is not very evident: is it the moon? is it the planet Venus?—They are very distant from us.

Be this as it may, if Nabonassar erected this edifice to serve for an observatory, it must at least be acknowledged that the Chaldeans had an observatory upwards of 2400 years before us. Let us now consider how many centuries were necessary for the slowness of human wit, to arrive at that pitch, which the erection of such a monument to the sciences must require.

The zodiac was invented in Chaldea, and not in Egypt. There appears to me three testimonies of weight: the first is, that the Chaldeans were an enlightened people, before Egypt, ever inundated by the Nile, could have been habit' able; the second that the signs of the zodiac correspond with the climate of Mesopotamia, and not with that of Egypt. The Egyptians could not have the sign of the bull in the month of April, since they do not work in this season: they could not in the month which we call August figure a sign by a maid laden with heads of corn, as their harvest is not at this time. They could not represent January by a pitcher of water, as it seldom rained in Egypt, and never in the

46

month of January. The third reason is, that the ancient signs of the Chaldean zodiac, were one of the articles of their religion. They were governed by twelve secondary gods, twelve mediating gods; each of them presiding over a constellation, as we are told by Diodorus Siculus (lib. 2.) The religion of the ancient Chaldeans was Sabism, that is to say, the adoration of one supreme God, and the veneration of the stars, and the celestial intelligences which presided over the stars. When they prayed, they turned themselves towards the northern star: so much analogy had their worship to astronomy.

Vitruvius in his ninth book, where he treats of solar quadrants, of the elevation of the sun, of the length of shadows, of the reflected light of the moon, constantly quotes the ancient Chaldeans, and not the Egyptians. This seems to me a proof sufficiently strong, that Chaldea and not Egypt, was considered as the cradle of that science; so that nothing is truer than that old Latin proverb

Tradidit Egyptis Babylon Egyptis Achivis.

XI

OF THE BABYLONIANS BECOME PERSIANS

THE PERSIANS were situated to the East of Babylon. They carried their arms and religion to Babylon, when Koresh, whom we call Cyrus, took that city, with the assistance of the Medes, who were established to the northward of Persia. We have two capital fables relating to Cyrus, that of Herodotus and that of Xenophon, which are in every respect contradictory, and which, nevertheless, a thousand different writers have copied.

Herodotus supposes a king of the Medes, that is to say, a king of Hyrcania, whom he calls Astyagus, a name derived from the Greek. This Hyrcanian Astyagus orders his grandson Cyrus to be drowned in his cradle, because he saw in his dream his daughter Mandane, mother to Cyrus, urinate so copiously, that she inundated all Asia. The rest of this adventure is nearly in the same style; this is a history of Gargantua, seriously written.

Xenophon makes the life of Cyrus a moral romance, nearly resembling our Telemachus. He begins by supposing, in order to recommend the masculine and robust education of his hero, that the Medes were voluptuaries sunk in effeminacy. Some inhabitants of Hyrcania, whom the Tartars then called the Scythians, had committed ravages for thirty years —were these Sybarites?

All that can be positively averred with respect to Cyrus, is that he was a great conqueror, and consequently a scourge of the earth. The basis of his history is very true: the episodes are fabulous: all histories are the same.

Rome existed in the time of Cyrus: her territories extended between four and five leagues, and she pillaged, as much as possible, her neighbors; but I would not support the battle of three Horatius's, the adventure of Lucretia, the bucklers descending from Heaven, nor the stone being cut with a razor. There were Jewish slaves in Babylon and elsewhere; but, humanly speaking, one might doubt that the angel Raphael had come down from Heaven to conduct young Tobit on foot towards Hyrcania, in order to receive some money, and to drive away the devil Asmodeus with the smoke of a pipe.

I shall take care not to touch upon the romance of Herodotus, or that of Xenophon, with respect to the life of Cyrus; but I shall observe that the Parsis, or Persians, pretended to have among them, for 6,000 years, an ancient zerdust, a prophet who had taught them to be just, and to revere the sun, as the ancient Chaldeans had revered the stars whilst they gazed upon them.

I shall take care not to affirm that these Persians and these Chaldeans were so just, or that I know so precisely at what time came their second zerdust, who rectified the worship of the sun, and taught them to adore only the God, author of the sun and the stars. He wrote, or rather commented upon, as it is said, the book of the Zend, which the Persians dispersed over Asia, now revered as their Bible: this book is, perhaps, the oldest in the world, after that of the five kings of the Chinese; it is written in the ancient, sacred language of the Chaldeans; and Mr. Hyde, who has given us a translation of the Sadder, would have procured us that of the Zend, had he been able to have defrayed the expense of such a search. I mean at least the Sadder, that extract of the Zend which is the catechism of the Persians. I there find that these Persians believed, for a long series of time, in a god, a devil, a resurrection, a paradise, a hell. They were, without contradiction, the first who framed these ideas: this was the most antique system, and which was not adopted by other nations, till after many ages; since the Pharisees among the Jews did not strongly maintain the immortality of the soul, and the dogma of rewards and punishments after death, till about the time of Herod.

This, perhaps, is the most important circumstance in the ancient history of the world. Here is an useful religion established upon the dogma of the immortality of the soul, and upon a knowledge of the creative being. Let us continue to observe how many degrees are necessary for the human understanding to pass through, in order to conceive such a system. Observe again that baptism and immersion into water, to purify the soul by the body, is one of the precepts of the Zend.

The origin of all rites is, perhaps, derived from the Persians and Chaldeans, and extended to the extremities of the west.

I shall not enter into an enquiry here, why and how the Babylonians had their secondary gods in acknowledging a sovereign god. This system, or rather this chaos, was that of all nations, except the tribunals of China. We every where find extreme folly united to a little wisdom in the laws, the worships, and customs; mankind is led more by instinct than reason; the divinity is every where adored and dishon' ored. The Persians revered statues as soon as they could procure sculptors: but even in these figures the symbols of immortality are discovered; we see heads soaring with wings to heaven, symbols of the emigration of a transitory life to that of immortality.

Let us now observe those customs, which are entirely human. I am astonished that Herodotus should say before all Greece, in his first book, that all the Babylonian women were compelled by the law to prostitute themselves once at least in their life to strangers, in the temple of Militia, or Venus. I am still more astonished that in all the histories which are compiled for the instruction of youth, this same tale is constantly preserved. This certainly must have been an elegant festival, a curious devotion, to see the dealers in camels, horses, oxen, and asses, repairing to church, and there descend to lie before the altar with the principal ladies of the city. Could such enormities be really practiced by a people who were esteemed polished? Is it possible that the magistrates of one of the greatest cities of the world should frame such a police? that the husbands should consent to prostitute their wives? that the fathers should abandon their daughters to the grooms of Asia? What is not in nature can never be true; I would as soon believe Dion. Cassius, who avers that the grave senators of Rome debated upon a decree, whereby Caesar, at the age of 57 years, should be allowed the privilege of enjoying all the women he chose.

Should not those who are at present employed in com'

piling ancient history, and copy so many authors without examining any of them, have perceived that either Herodotus related fables, or rather that his text was corrupted, and that he only meant those courtesans who are settled in all great cities, and who even waited for passengers upon the roads.

I shall give no more credit to Sextus Empiricus, who pretends that pederasty was ordered among the Persians. What a pity! How can it be suggested that a law was enacted by men, the execution of which would have destroyed the human race? Pederasty was, on the contrary, expressly forbidden in the book of Zend, which may be seen in the abridgment of the Sadder, where it is said, (port 9) "That there is no greater sin."

Strabo says that the Persians married their mothers—but what vouchers does he produce? hearsays and idle reports: these may furnish an epigram for Catullus. *Num magus ex matre & nato nascatur aportet.* Every magus is to be born from the incestuous intercourse of a mother and her son. Such a law is incredible; an epigram is no proof. If there had been no mothers inclinable to lie with their sons, there would consequently have been no priests among the Persians. The religion of the magi, the great object of which was population, should rather have allowed fathers to cohabit with their daughters, than for mothers to have laid with their sons, as an old man might have begot something, but an old woman was debarred this advantage.

In a word, when we read history, we should constantly be upon our guard not to adopt fables.

XII

OF SYRIA

BY ALL the monuments which remain for our inspection, I find that the country which extends from Alexandretta or Scanderoon, as far as Bagdat, was always called Syria; the alphabet used by this people was always Syriac: that the ancient cities of Zobah, Balbec, and Damascus, were here situated, and afterwards those of Antiochus, Seleucia, and Palmyra. Balk was so ancient, that the Persians pretend that their Bram or Abraham came from Balk amongst them: where then could that ancient empire of Assyria, of which so much has been said, be situated, if it was not in the land of fables?

The Gauls at one time extended themselves as far as the Rhine; at other times, they were more confined; but who could ever think of placing a vast empire between the Rhine and the Gauls? Or that the nations bordering upon the Euphrates were called Assyrians, when they extended themselves towards Damascus; and the people of Syria were called Assyrians, when they approached the Euphrates? the difficulty may be reduced to the discussion of this single point. All the neighboring nations have intermingled; they were each of them at war and exchanged their limits. But when once capital cities are erected, these cities establish a certain distinction between the two nations. Thus the Babylonians, whether conquerors or conquered, were always a different people from that of Syria: the ancient characters of the Syriac language, were not the same with those of the ancient Chaldeans.

The worship, the superstition, the laws, whether good or bad, the extravagant customs, were none of them similar. The goddess of Syria of such great antiquity, was no way related to the worship of the Chaldeans. The magi of the Chaldeans, the Babylonians and the Persians, never made themselves eunuchs, as did the priests of the goddess of Syria; what a strange opposition, the Syrians revered the figure of the god whom we call Priapus, and the priests dispossessed themselves of their virility!

Does not this renunciation to generation evince great antiquity—considerable population? It is impossible that such attacks should be made upon nature in a country where the species was scarce.

The priests of Cybele in Phrygia made themselves eunuchs in the same manner as those of Syria. Once more, can it be doubted that this was not the effect of ancient custom for men to sacrifice to the gods what was the dearest to them, and not to expose themselves before beings whom they thought pure, to accidents which they judged were impure? Is it astonishing after such sacrifices, that among other people a sacrifice should be made of the prepuce; or that among some of the African nations, they should in the same manner offer up a testicle? The fables of Atis and Combalus are mere fables, like that of Jupiter, who made a eunuch of his father Saturn: superstition gives birth to ridic-

54

ulous customs, and the spirit of romance ascribes a thousand absurd reasons for them.

What I shall farther observe of the ancient Syrians, is that the city which has since been called the holy city, and by the Greeks Hierapolis, was by the Syrians named Magog. The word Mag has a great affinity with the ancient Magi, it seems to have been in common applied to all those who were in those climates consecrated to the service of the divinity: every people had a holy city. We know that Thebes in Egypt was the city of god; Babylon was the city of god; and Apameus in Phrygia was also the city of god.

The Hebrews, a long time after, make mention of the people of Gog and Magog; they might by these names signify the people of the Euphrates and the Orontes; they might also signify the Scythians, who ravaged Asia before the time of Cyrus, and who made deviations in Phenicia. But it is of little importance to know what idea a Jew framed to himself when he uttered the words Gog or Magog.

I do not, in other respects, hesitate believing that the Syrians were much more ancient than the Egyptians, for this evident reason, that the lands which are most easily cultivated, are necessarily the first people, and the earliest in a flourishing state.

XIII

OF THE PHOENICIANS AND SANCHONIATON

THE PHOENICIANS were probably united as a body of people, as early as the other inhabitants of Syria. They may not be so ancient as the Chaldeans, because their country is not so fertile: Sidon, Tyre, Joppa, Berith, and Ascalon, are barren lands. Maritime trade has constantly been the last resource of every people. They began by cultivating their land before they built ships to go in search of other countries beyond the sea. But those who are compelled to yield to maritime trade are soon possessed of that industry, the daughter of necessity, which does not animate other nations. There is no mention made of any maritime expeditions, either among the Chaldeans or the Indians. Even the Egyptians looked with horror upon the sea; the sea was their Typhon, an evil-disposed being; and this makes the four hundred ships that were fitted out by Sesostris for the conquest of India, very questionable; but the enterprises of the Phoenicians are real. Carthage and Cadiz founded by them, the discovery of England, their trade to India conducted by Eziongaber, their manufactures of valuable stuffs, their art of dying purple, testify their abilities, and those abilities caused their grandeur.

The Phoenicians were with respect to antiquity, what the Venetians were in the fifteenth century, and what the

Dutch have since been, compelled to enrich themselves by industry.

Commerce necessarily required registers, which supplied the place of our account books, with easy and lasting signs to fix those registers. The opinion which supposes that the Phoenicians were the authors of the written alphabet, is therefore very probable. I shall not aver that they invented such characters before the Chaldeans; but their alphabet was certainly the most complete and useful, as they expressed the vowels, which the Chaldeans did not. The word Alpha-bet itself, composed of their two first characters, is an evi-dence in favor of the Phoenicians.

I do not find that the Egyptians ever communicated their letters or their language to any other people: on the other hand, the Phoenicians imparted their language and their al-phabet to the Carthaginians, who afterwards changed them. Their letters were transformed into those of the Greeks; what a prejudice in favor of the antiquity of the Phoenicians!

Sanchoniaton, the Phoenician, who wrote long before the Tuscan war, the history of the first ages, some of whose fragments, translated by Eusebius, have been handed down to us by Philo de Biblos; Sanchoniaton, I say, informs us that the Phoenicians had sacrificed from time immemorial to the elements and the winds; this indeed agrees with the dis-positions of a maritime people. He was desirous in his history to trace things to their origin, like all the primitive writers: he was animated with the same ambition as the authors of the Zend and the Vedam, the same ambition as Manethian in Egypt, and Hesiod in Greece.

What proves the prodigious antiquity of the book of

Sanchoniaton is, that the first lines of it were read in the celebration of the mysteries of Isis and Ceres, a homage which the Egyptians and Greeks would not have paid to a foreign author, if he had not been considered as one of the first sources of human knowledge.

Sanchoniaton wrote nothing of himself, he consulted all the ancient archives, and particularly the priest Jerombal. The name of Sanchoniaton signifies, in the ancient Phenician, *A lover of truth*. Porphyrus, Theodoret, and Eusebius, acknowledge it. Phenicia was called the country of the Archives, Kirjath Sepher. When the Hebrews settled in a part of this country, they gave him his testimony, as we find in Joshua and the book of Judges.

Jerombal, whom Sanchoniaton consulted, was a priest of the supreme God, whom the Phenicians named Jaho, Jehovah, a reputed sacred name, adopted by the Egyptians, and afterwards by the Jews. We find by the fragments of this monument, which is of such antiquity, that Tyre had for a great length of time existed, though it was not yet become a powerful city.

The word El, which signified god among the first Phenicians, has some analogy to the Alla of the Arabians; and it is probable, that the Greeks composed their Elios from this monosyllable El. But what is most observable, is, that we find the ancient Phenicians had the word Eloa, Eloim, which the Hebrews for a very long time afterwards retained, when they settled in Canaan.

The Jews derived all the names they gave to God, Eloa, Iaho, Adonaï, from Phenicia: this cannot be otherwise, as

58

the Jews in Canaan did not for a great while speak any thing but the Phenician tongue.

The word Iaho, that ineffable word with the Jews, and which they never pronounced, was so common in the east, that Diodorus in his second book, speaking of those who feigned conversations with the gods, says, that "Minos boasted of having communed with the god Zeus, Zamolxis with the goddess Vesta, and the Jew Moses with the god Iaho," etc.

What deserves particular observation, is that Sanchonia-ton, in relating the ancient cosmology of his country, speaks at first of the chaos enveloped in dark air, *chaut ereb*. Erebus, Hesiod's night, is derived from the Phenician word, which the Greeks preserved. From chaos came Muth or Moth, which signified matter; now who discovered this matter? It was Colpi Jaho, the spirit of God, the wind of God, or rather the mouth of God, the voice of God. By the voice of God animals and men were created.

We may easily be convinced that this cosmogony, is the origin of almost all the others. The more ancient people are always imitated by those who succeed them; they acquire their language, they follow part of their rites, and they adopt their antiquities and fables. I am sensible how obscure are all the origins of the Chaldeans, the Syrians, the Pheni-cians, the Egyptians, and the Greeks. What origin is not so? We can know nothing certain concerning the formation of the world, but what the Creator of the world has deigned to teach us himself. We walk with security, till we reach certain limits; we know that Babylon existed before Rome; that the cities of Syria were powerful before Jerusalem was

59

known; that there were kings of Egypt before Jacob or Abraham: we know what societies have been the last established; but to know with precision which was the first people, a revelation is absolutely necessary.

We are at least allowed to weigh probabilities, and to make use of our reason in what does not relate to our sacred dogmas, which are superior to all reason.

It is very strongly attested that the Phenicians inhabited for a long time their country, before the Hebrews made their appearance there. Could the Hebrews learn the Phenician tongue when they were wandering at a distance from Phenicia, in the desert, in the midst of some Arabian bands?

Could the Phenician tongue have become the common language of the Hebrews, and could they have written in that language in the time of Joshua, amidst continual devastations and massacres? Did not the Hebrews after Joshua, when they had been for a long while in a state of bondage, in the very country they had sacked and burnt; did they not then acquire some small knowledge of the language of their masters, as they did a little of the Chaldean, when they were slaves at Babylon?

Is it not highly probable that a trading, industrious, and learned people, settled from time immemorial, and who were the reputed inventors of letters, should write long before a wandering people, newly settled in their neighborhood, without any knowledge, without any industry, without any trade, subsisting solely by rapine?

Can the authenticity of Sanchoniaton preserved by Eusebius be seriously denied? or can it be imagined with the learned Hewit that Sanchoniaton borrowed from Moses?

When all the remains of the monuments of antiquity intimate that Sanchoniaton lived about the time of Moses,
nothing can be determined; the intelligent and judicious
reader is to decide between Hewit and Vandale, who refuted
him. We are in search of truth and not disputation.

XIV

OF THE SCYTHIANS AND GOMERANS

LET US leave Gomer just after coming out of the arch to go and subjugate Gaul, and in a few years people it: let us leave Tubal to go into Spain, and Magog into the north of Germany, about the time that the son of Cham produced an amazing number of children completely black, towards Guinea and Congo. These disgusting impertinences have been obtruded in so many books, that they are not worth mentioning; children begin to ridicule them. But by what weakness, or by what secret malignity, or by what affectation to display ill-placed eloquence, have so many historians made such great eulogiae upon the Scythians, whom they knew nothing of?

Why does Quintus Curtius, in talking of the Scythians, who were situated to the north of Sogdia, beyond the Oxus (which he mistakes for the Tanais, fifty leagues distant) why, I say, did Quintus Curtius put a philosophical harangue into the mouth of those Barbarians? why does he imagine that they reproached Alexander with his thirst of conquest? why does he make them say, that Alexander is the most famous robber upon the earth, those who had practiced rapine all over Asia, so long before him? why, in fine, does Quintus Curtius represent these Scythians as the justest of men? The reason is, that placing the Tanais towards the

62

Caspian sea, like a bad geographer, he speaks declamatorily of the supposed disinterestedness of the Scythians.

If Horace, in contrasting the manners of the Scythians to those of the Romans, gives an harmonious panegyric upon those barbarians. If he says,

> Campestreo milias Scithae
> Quorum plaustra vagas rite trahunt domos
> Vivunt & rigidi Getae;
>
> Happy the Scythians, houseless train!
> Who roll their vagrant dwellings o'er the plain;
> Happy the Getes, fierce and brave;

it is that Horace speaks as a poet somewhat satirical, who is willing to honor strangers at the expense of his own country.

For the same reason Tacitus exhausts himself in the praise of the barbarous Germans, who pillaged the Gauls, and immolated men to their abominable Gods. Tacitus, Quintus Curtius, and Horace, are like those pedagogues, who, in order to excite an emulation in their disciples, are lavish of their praises before them of strange children, however unworthy of their applause.

The Scythians are those same Barbarians, whom we have since called Tartars: they are the same who long before Alexander repeatedly ravaged Asia, and have been the depredators of a great part of the continent. At one time bearing the name of Monguls or Huns, they subjected China and Judea; at another, under the name of Turks, they drove out the Arabs, who had conquered part of Asia. From these extensive plains the Huns went forth in order to reach Rome.

63

These are the disinterested and just men, whose equity our compilers so highly celebrate when they copy Quintus Cur-tius. In this manner are we pestered with ancient histories, without choice and without judgment; they are read with nearly the same kind of taste as they are written, and the natural offspring of this sort of erudition must be error.

The Ruffians at this time inhabit the ancient European Scythia: this people have furnished history with some very astonishing facts. There have been revolutions upon earth that have more struck the imagination; but there are none that give so much satisfaction to the human mind, and do it so much honor as this. Conquerors and devastations have made their appearance; but that a single man should, in the course of twenty years, change the manners, the laws, and the sentiments of the greatest empire upon earth; that all the arts should have flocked together to embellish deserts, is really worthy of admiration. A woman, who could neither read nor write, brought to perfection the work which Peter began; another woman, named Elizabeth, extended still far-ther those noble essays. Another empress has gone beyond either of the two former; her subjects have imbibed her genius; the revolutions of the palace have not retarded a single moment the progress of the empire towards felicity. In a word, half a century has more enlightened the court of Scythia, than ever were Greece and Rome.

XV

OF ARABIA

THOSE WHO are curious about such monuments as those of Egypt, need not, I imagine, go in search of them to Arabia. Mecca, it is said, was built about the time of Abraham; but it is situated in so sandy and barren a soil, that it does not appear this city could have been settled before those which were founded near rivers, in fertile countries. Above half of Arabia is a vast desert, either sandy or stony; but Arabia Felix deserved that name, as, being surrounded with thick woods and a tempestuous sea, it was sheltered from the rapacity of robbers, who, till the time of Mahomet, were called conquerors; or rather, as it was the boundaries of his victories. This advantage is far above its aromatics, its incense, its cinnamon (which is middling) or even its coffee, which now creates its riches.

Arabia Deserta is that unhappy country inhabited by some Amalekites, Moabites, and Midianites; a shocking country, which does not now contain above nine or ten thou-sant wandering Arabian robbers, and which could not furnish subsistence for more. It was in these deserts that, it is said, two millions of Hebrews remained for forty years. This is not the true Arabia; and this country is often called the desert of Syria.

Arabia Petraea is thus called only from the name of

65

Petra, a small fortress, to which the Arabs certainly did not give this name, but which received it from the Greeks, about the time of Alexander. This Arabia Petraea is very small, and may, without doing it prejudice, be confounded with Arabia Deserta: they have each been constantly inhabited by bands of vagabonds.

As to that extensive part called Happy, half of it con-sists also in deserts; but upon advancing some miles into the interior parts, either to the east of Moca, or to the east of Mecca, there is found the most pleasant country in the world. The air is continually perfumed, during a perpetual summer, by the odor of the aromatic plants which nature spontaneously produces. Thousands of streams flow from the mountains, and preserve an incessant coolness, which moderates the heat of the sun beneath ever-green shades.

It was particularly in this country, that the words garden and paradise implied celestial favor.

The gardens of Saana, towards Aden, were more fa-mous among the Arabians, than were those of Alcinous among the Greeks. And this Aden or Eden was called the spot of delight: an ancient Shedad is still spoken of, whose gardens were not in less renown. Shade in those scorching climates was considered as happiness.

This vast country of Yemen is so fine, its ports are so happily situated upon the Indian ocean, that it is said Alex-ander was desirous of conquering Yemen, in order to make it the seat of his empire, and the emporium of trade for the whole world. He would have preserved the ancient canal of the kings of Egypt, which joined the Nile to the Red Sea; and all the treasures of India would have been transplanted from Aden or Eden, to his city of Alexandria. Such an enterprise bears no resemblance to those insipid and absurd fables with which all ancient history is replete. He must indeed have subjugated all Arabia: if any one could have done it, Alexander must have been he. But it seems that this people did not fear him; they did not even send deputies to him, when Egypt and Persia had submitted to his yoke.

The Arabians, whose defense are their deserts and their courage, have never submitted to a foreign yoke. Trajan conquered only a small part of Arabia Petraea: they to this time brave the power of the Turk. This great people have always been as free as Scythians, and more civilized.

Care should be taken not to confound these ancient Arabs with that banditti, who said they were descended from Ishmael. The Ishmaelites or Agareans, or those who called themselves the children of Cethura, were foreign tribes, who never set foot in Arabia Felix. Their bands wandered in Arabia Petraea towards the country of Madia; they afterwards intermingled with the true Arabians in the time of Mahomet, when they embraced his religion.

Those may be properly called the people of Arabia, who were the real aborigines, that is to say, who from time immemorial inhabited this fine country, without intermixing with any other nation, without having ever been conquered or conquerors. Their religion was the most natural and simple of any; it consisted in worshipping a god, and venerating the stars, which seemed, under so fine and clear a sky, to set forth the grandeur of God, with more magnificence than any other part of nature. They considered the planets as mediators between god and men: they followed this religion till

67

the time of Mahomet. I believe they were addicted to many superstitions, as they were men; but detached from the rest of the world by seas and deserts, in the possession of a delicious country, above every want and fear, they must necessarily have been less prone to wickedness, and not so superstitious as other nations.

They were never known to invade the property of their neighbors, like famished carnivorous animals; nor to devour the weak, under pretense of divine ordinances; nor to pay their court to the powerful, by flattering them with false oracles. Their superstition was neither absurd nor barbarous.

They are not mentioned in our universal histories, fabricated in our western part of the globe. I really believe they had no connection with that little Jewish nation, which is become the object and foundation of our pretended universal histories, wherein a certain kind of authors copy one from the other, whilst they all forget three-fourths of the earth.

XVI

OF BRAM, ABRAM, OR ABRAHAM

IT SEEMS that the name of Bram, Abram, Abraham, or Ibrahim, was one of the most common names with the an-cient people of Asia. The Indians, whom we look upon as one of the first nations, make their Brama a son of God, who taught the Bramins the manner of adoring him. This name came gradually into veneration. The Arabians, the Chaldeans, the Persians, all used it, and the Jews looked upon him as one of their patriarchs. The Arabs, who traded with the Indians, were perhaps the first who had some con-fused idea of Brama, whom they called Abrama, and from whom they afterwards boasted of being descended. The Chaldeans adopted him as a legislator; the Persians called their ancient religion, Millat Ibrahim; the Medes, Kish Ibra-him. They supposed that this Ibrahim, or Abraham, was born in Bactria, and that he resided near the city Balk; they revered in him a prophet of the religion of ancient Zoroaster: he belonged doubtless, only to the Hebrews, as they acknowl-edge him for their father in their sacred books.

Some of the learned have thought that it was an Indian name, because the Indian priests called themselves Bramins or Brachmanes; and that several of their sacred institutions have an immediate affinity with this name: whereas, among the western Asiatics no institution can be traced, which derives its name from Abram or Abraham. There never was any Abramic society; no rite or ceremony of this name: but as the Jewish books say that Abraham was the stock of the Hebrew race, they should be credited without hesitation.

The Alcoran quotes the Arabian histories, with regard to Abraham, but very little is said about him: according to those historians, he was the founder of Mecca.

The Jews make him come from Chaldea, and not from India or Bactria; they were in the neighborhood of Chaldea; India and Bactria were unknown to them: Abraham was a stranger to all these people, and Chaldea being a country long famed for arts and sciences, it was an honor, humanly speaking, for a small nation inclosed in Palestine, to reckon among the number of their ancestors an ancient sage, a reputed Chaldean.

If it be allowable to examine the historical part of the Judaical books, by the same rules as are followed in the criticisms of other histories, it must be agreed with all commentators, that the recital of the adventures of Abraham, as it is found in the Pentateuch, would be liable to many difficulties, if it were found in another history.

According to Genesis Abraham came out of Haran at the age of seventy-five, after the death of his father.

But it is said in the same Genesis that Thareus his father having had children at the age of seventy, he lived to be two hundred and five years old; so that Abraham was a hundred and thirty-five years old when he came from Chaldea. It appears strange, that at such an age he should abandon the fertile country of Mesopotamia, to go three hundred miles from thence, in the barren rocky country of Sichem, where no trade was carried on. He is made to go from Sichem to Memphis, which are about six hundred miles distant, to purchased corn; and upon his arrival, the king becomes enamoured with his wife, who is seventy-five years old.

I do not enter upon the divine part of this history, I keep close to my researches into antiquity. It is said that Abraham received considerable presents from the king of Egypt. This country was from that time a powerful state; the monarchy was founded, and arts were therefore cultivated; the flood was stopped; canals were dug on every side to receive its inundations, without which the country would not have been habitable.

Now, I ask any reasonable man, whether ages were not required to establish such an empire in a country which had been for a length of time inaccessible and laid waste by the very waters which rendered it fertile? Abraham, according to Genesis, arrived in Egypt two thousand years before our vulgar era. The Manetons, Herodotuses, Diodoruses, Eratostheneses, and many others are to be forgiven, when they allow the kingdom of Egypt to be of such amazing antiquity; and this antiquity must have been very modern, in comparison of that of the Chaldeans and Syrians.

May it be allowable to examine a passage in the history of Abraham? He is represented upon his going out of Egypt as a Nomadian pastor, wandering between mount Carmel and the lake of Asphaltides: this is the most barren desert of all Arabia Petraea. His tents are conveyed thither by three hundred and eighteen domestics, and Lot, his nephew, is settled in the borough of Sodom. A king of Babylon, a king

71

of Persia, a king of Pontus, and kings of several other nations, league together to wage war against Sodom, and four other little neighboring boroughs. They take these boroughs and Sodom. Lot is their prisoner. It is not easy to comprehend how five such great and powerful kings should league together to make an attack, in that manner, upon a band of Arabs, in such a savage corner of the earth; or how Abraham defeated such powerful monarchs with only three hundred and eighteen country valets, or how he could pursue them beyond Damascus. Some translators have wrote Dan for Damascus; but Dan did not exist in the time of Moses, much less in the time of Abraham. Lake Asphaltides, where Sodom was situated, was more than three hundred miles distant from Damascus: all this is above our comprehension. Everything is miraculous in the history of the Hebrews; we have already said it, and we again repeat it, that we believe these prodigies, and all the others, without examining them.

XVII

OF INDIA

IF CONJECTURES are allowable, the Indians toward the Ganges are, perhaps, the men who were the most anciently united into a body of people. It is certain that the soil, where animals most easily find pasture, is soon covered with that species, which it is fit to nourish.

Now there is no country in the world where the human species have within their reach more wholesome and agreeable ailments, or in greater plenty, than towards the Ganges; rice grows spontaneously; pineapples, cocoa, dates, and fig trees, offer on every side delicious regales; the orange and lemon trees at once yield refreshing liquor and some nourishment; sugar-canes are under their very hand; the palm and broad-leaf fig-trees spread the thickest shade. There is no occasion in this country to skin herds, to defend their children against the inclemency of the season; they are to this hour brought up to the age of puberty quite naked. Life was here never risqued for the means of preserving it, by attacking animals in order to feed upon their dismembered joints, as has been practised every where else.

Men would of themselves have united into society in this happy climate; no contest would have arisen for a parched country to rear bands of negroes: war would not have been waged for a well or a fountain, as with the Barbarians of Arabia Petraea.

73

I shall make no mention here of the ancient monuments of which the Bramins boast: it is sufficient to know that the most antique rarities which the emperor of China, Camhi, had in his palace, were Indian: he displayed to our mathe- matical missionaries Indian specie in coin of much earlier date than any of the copper money of the Chinese emperors; and it was, probably, from the Indians that the kings of Persia acquired the art of coining.

The Greeks, before the time of Pythagoras, travelled into India for instruction. The signs of the seven planets and of the seven metals are still almost all over the earth, such as the Indians invented: the Arabians were obliged to adopt their cyphers. Those of games, which do the greatest honor to the human understanding, incontestibly come from India; as elephants, for which we have substituted towers, evince. In fine, the people who were the earliest known, the Persians, Phenicians, Arabians, Egyptians, went from time immemo- rial to traffic in India, in order to bring home spices, which nature has given to those climates alone; but the Indians never went to ask any thing from other nations.

One Bacchus is mentioned, who is said to have set out from Egypt, or a country west of Asia, to conquer India. This Bacchus, whoever he was, must therefore have known that there was, at the end of our continent, a nation more valuable than his own. Want created the first robbers; they invaded India for no other reason but because it was rich; and surely a rich people is united, civilized, and polished, long before a society of thieves.

What strikes me the most in India, is that ancient opinion of the transmigration of souls, which in time extended itself

74

as far as China, and into Europe. Not that the Indians knew what a soul was; but they imagined that this principle, whether it was aerial or igneous, successively animated different bodies. Let us attentively observe that system of philosophy which relates to morals. The dread of being condemned by Visnon and Brama, to become the most vile and unhappy of animals, was a great constraint upon those of a perverse disposition. We shall presently find that all the great people had an idea of another life, though their notions of it were different. I meet with very few amongst the ancient empires, except the Chinese, who did not establish the doctrine of the immortality of the soul. Their first legislators promulgated only moral laws; they thought it sufficient to exhort men to virtue, and to compel them by a severe police.

The doctrine of the metempsychosis imposed another constraint upon the Indians; the dread of killing their father or their mother, in slaying men and animals, inspired them with horror for murder and all violence, which became amongst them a second nature. Thus all the Indians, whose families are not allied, either to the Arabians or the Tartars, are to this hour the mildest of men. Their religion, and the temperature of their climate, rendered these people entirely similar to those peaceable animals which we rear in our folds and dovehouses, to destroy them at pleasure. All ferocious nations who descended from the mounts Caucasus, Taurus, and Imaus, to subjugate the inhabitants of the coasts of the Indies, the Hydaspes, and the Ganges, conquered them by only appearing.

The same thing would happen now to those primitive Christians called Quakers, who are as pacific as the Indians;

75

they would be devoured by other nations, if they were not protected by their warlike countrymen. The Christian religion, which these alone strictly follow, is as much an enemy to blood as that of the Pythagorians. But the Christian people have never observed their religion, and the ancient Indian casts always practiced theirs; because Pythagorianism is the only religion in the world which could render the horror of murder part of filial piety, and a religious sentiment. The transmigration of souls is a system so simple, and even so probable to the eyes of ignorant people; it is so easy to believe that what animates one man may afterwards animate another, that all those who adopted this religion, imagined that they saw the souls of their relations in all the men that surrounded them: they believed that they were all brothers, fathers, mothers, and children of one another. This idea necessarily inspired universal charity; a man trembled at wounding a being who was of the same family: in a word, the ancient religion of India, and that of the literary men in China, are the only ones, wherein men have not been barbarous. How could it afterwards happen that these same men, who looked upon killing an animal as a crime, should allow the women to burn themselves upon their husbands' dead bodies, in the vain hope of being born again in bodies that should be more beautiful and more happy? Because fanaticism and contradiction are the appendages to human nature.

It should be particularly observed, that abstinence from the flesh of animals, is a necessary consequence of the climate; meat is soon corrupted by its extreme heat and humidity, and is therefore a very bad ailment. Strong liquors are also forbidden, by the necessity of drinking cooling liquors in India. The metempsychosis reached, indeed, our northern countries. The Celts thought that they should regenerate in other bodies; but if the Druids had subjoined to this doctrine a prohibition of eating flesh, they would not have been obeyed.

We scarce know any thing of the rites of the ancient Bramins, which are still preserved. The books of the Hanscri, which they have still in this ancient sacred language, give us but very little insight into them. Their Vedams have been as long unknown as the Zend of the Persians, and the Five Kings of the Chinese. It is scarce six score years since the Europeans had the first notion of the Five Kings; and the Zend was never seen but by the celebrated Dr. Hyde, who had not wherewithal to purchase it, nor to pay the inter-preter; and by the trader Chardin, who would not give the price for it he was asked. We had no other extract of the Zend but the Sadder, which I have amply spoke of.

The library of Paris has, by a mere lucky accident, procured an ancient book of the Bramins: this is the Ezourvedam, written before the expedition of Alexander into India, with a recital of all the ancient rites of the Brachmanes, intitled the Cormovedam. This manuscript, which is translated by a Bramin, is not really the Vedam itself, but it is a sequel of the rites and opinions contained in that law. We may, therefore, flatter ourselves that we have a knowledge of the three most ancient writings in the world.

We can never hope to have any thing from the Egyptians, their books are lost, their religion is annihilated; they no longer undestand their own vulgar tongue, still less the

sacred one: so that which was nearer to us, more easily preserved, and deposited in immense libraries, is lost for ever;
and we have found, at the end of the world, monuments not
less authentic, which we had no reason to expect finding.

The truth and authenticity of this ritual of the Brach-
mans, of which I am speaking, cannot be doubted. The
author certainly does not batter his sect; he does not attempt
to disguise their superstitions, or to give them an air of probability, by feigned explanations, or to excuse them by allegories. He gives an account of the most extravagant laws,
with simplicity and candor; human understanding appears
then in all its misery. If the Bramins observed all the laws
of their Vedam, there is no monk who would submit to
such a state; scarce is the son of a Bramin born before he
is the slave of ceremonies: his tongue is rubbed with rosin
mixed with flour; the word Oum is pronounced; twenty
divinities are invoked before his navel skin is cut; but these
words are repeated to him, Live to command Men; and
as soon as he can speak, he is taught the dignity of his being.
The Brachmanes were, in effect, for a long time sovereigns
of India; and theocracy was established in that vast country
more than in any country in the world.

The infant is soon exposed to the moon; the supreme
being is implored to efface those sins which the child may
have committed, though he has been born only eight days;
anthems are sung to fires; the child, after a hundred ceremonies, is called Chormo, which is the honorary title of the
Bramins.

As soon as the child can walk, his life is passed in bath-
ing and repeating prayers. He sacrifices for the dead; and

78

this sacrifice is instituted, that Brama may give to the souls of the child's ancestors an agreeable abode in other bodies.

The five winds that may issue from the five openings of the human body, are prayed to. This is not more strange than the prayers which are repeated to the god Crepitum, by the good old women of Rome.

There is no function of nature, no action among the Bramins, without prayers. The first time that the child's head is shaved, the father says to the razor, very devoutly, "Razor, shave my son as thou hast shaved the sun and the god Indro." It is possible that the god Indro might formerly have been shaved; but as to the sun's undergoing that opera' tion, this is not very easy to comprehend, unless the Bramins have had our Apollo, whom we still represent without a beard.

The recital of all these ceremonies would be as tedious as they appear ridiculous; and in their blind state, they say as much of ours: but there is a mystery amongst them, which should not be passed over in silence: this is, the Matricha Machom; this mystery gives fresh being and new life.

The soul is supposed to be in the breast, and this, indeed, is the sentiment of almost all antiquity. The hand is moved from the breast to the head, in pressing upon the nerve which we imagine communicates from one of these organs to the other, and in this manner the soul is conducted to the brain. When it is certain that the soul is well hung, the young man then calls out, that his soul and body are united to the supreme being, and says, "I am myself part of the divinity."

This opinion was that of the most respectable philosophers of Greece, of those Stoics who have raised human nature above itself, that of the divine Antoninus's; and it must be owned that nothing was more capable of inspiring great virtues: to believe one's self part of the divinity, is to impose a law of doing nothing that is not worthy of God himself.

We find in this law the Brachmanes' ten commandments, and these are ten sins to be avoided; they are divided into three species, the sins of the body, those of the word, and those of the will. To strike or kill one's neighbor, to rob him, and violate a woman, these are bodily sins; dissimulation, lying, and scandal, are the sins of the world; those of the will consist in evil-wishing, in being envious of others' good, in not being affected with others' misfortunes. These ten commandments make us forgive all the ridiculous rites. We evidently find that morality is the same with all civilized nations; and that the most sacred customs amongst one people, appear to others as extravagant or detestable. Established rites at present divide mankind, and morality re-unites them.

Superstition never prevented the Brachmanes from acknowledging an only God. Strabo, in his fifteenth book, says that they adore a supreme god; that they remain silent for several years, before they dare speak; that they are sober, chaste, and temperate; that justice guides their life, and they die without remorse. This is corroborated by St. Clement of Alexandria, Apuleius, Porphyry, Paladius, and St. Ambrose. We should constantly remember that they enjoyed a terrestrial paradise, and that those who abused God's bounties were driven out of that paradise.

The fall of degenerated man is the foundation of the theology of almost all nations. The natural bias of man to complain of the present, and praise the past, has made it universally believed, that there was a golden age, to which the iron ages have succeeded. What is still more extraordinary, is, that the Vedam of the ancient Brachmanes taught that the first man was Adimo and the first woman Procriti: Adimo, signified lord, and Procriti meant life; as Hera, among the Phenicians and the Hebrews, signified also life, or the serpent. This conformity deserves great attention.

XVIII

OF CHINA

DARE WE speak of the Chinese, without having recourse to their own annals? They are confirmed by the unanimous opinion of our travellers of different sects, Jacobins, Jesuits, Lutherans, Calvinists, all interested in contradicting them. It is evident, that the empire of China was formed upwards of four thousand years ago. This people of antiquity never heard any mention made of those physical revolutions, of those inundations, those fiery devastations, the slight remembrance of which is preserved and changed in the fables of the deluge of Deucalion, and the fall of Phaeton. The climate of China was therefore preserved from these scourges, as it always was from the plague, literally speaking, which has made such frequent ravages in Africa, Asia, and Europe.

If any annals carry with them the stamp of certainty, they are those of China, which have united, as has been already said, the history of heaven with that of earth. Singular from every other people, they have constantly marked their epochas by eclipses, and the conjunctions of the planets; and our astronomers, who have examined their calculations, have been surprised to find them almost all just. Other nations invented allegorical fables, and the Chinese wrote their history with the pen and the astrolabe in their hand, with such simplicity as cannot be equalled in the rest of Asia.

82

Each reign of their emperors was written by contempo-
raries; there are no different methods of reckoning amongst
them, no contradictory chronologies. Our travelling missionaries candidly relate, that when they spoke to the wife
emperor Camhi, of the chronology of the Vulgate, of the
Septuagint, and the Samaritan, Camhi replied to them, is
it possible that the books you believe in are at variance?

The Chinese wrote upon thin tablets of bamboo, when
the Chaldeans did not yet write upon anything but bricks;
and they have still some ancient tablets, which their varnishes
have preserved from rotting. These are perhaps the most
ancient monuments in the world. They have no history before that of their emperors, no fictions, no prodigies, no inspired men, who called themselves demi-gods, as with the
Egyptians and Greeks: when these people write, they write
reasonably.

They particularly differ from other nations in their history, making no mention of a college of priests, who ever
controlled their laws. The Chinese do not refer to those
savage times, when it was necessary for men to be cheated
in order to be guided. Other people began their history by
the origin of the world; the Zend of the Persians, the Vedam
of the Indians, Sanchoniaton, Manetho; in fine, down to
Hesiod, they all trace things back to their origin and the
formation of the world. The Chinese have not been guilty
of this folly; their history comprehends no other than historical times.

In this place above all others, we should apply our great
principle, that a nation whose first chronicles attest the existence of a vast empire, powerful and wise, must have been

assembled as a body of people for antecedent ages. Here is a people, who, for upwards of four thousand years, daily write their annals. Again, would it not be madness to disbelieve that to be expert in all the arts necessary to society, even so far as to write, and to write well, more time was necessary than the Chinese empire has subsisted, in reckoning only from the emperor Tohi, till now? None of the literati of China doubt that the Five Kings existed two thousand three hundred years before our vulgar era. This monument, then, is four hundred years anterior to the first Babylonian observations sent into Greece by Calisthenes. Does it really become the literati of Paris to contest the antiquity of a Chinese book, considered as authentic by all the tribunals of China?

The first rudiments of every kind are always slower in their progress than the more advanced stages. Let us constantly remember, that five hundred years ago scarce any one knew how to write, either in the North, in Germany or France. Those tallies, which bakers still use, were our hieroglyphics, and our books of account. There is no other kind of arithmetic used in collecting the taxes; and the name of tallies are still a proof of it in the country. Our capricious customs, which were not revised by writing, till within these four hundred and fifty years, sufficiently teach us how scarce the art of writing then was. There are no people in Europe, who have not latterly made more progress within half a century in all the arts, than they had made from the time of the invasions of the Barbarians, till the fourteenth century.

I shall not here examine why the Chinese, who were ar-

84

rived at the knowledge and practice of every thing that was useful in society, did not go as far as we do at present in the sciences: they are, I allow, as bad physicians as we were two hundred years ago, and as the Greeks and Romans; but they brought morality to perfection, which is the first of the sciences.

Their vast and populous empire was already governed like a family, whose monarch was the father; and forty of whose legislative tribunals were considered as the elder brothers, whilst we were wandering in the forest of the Ardennes.

Their religion was simple, wise, august, free from all superstition and all barbarity, ere we had yet Theutats, to whom the Druids sacrificed the children of our ancestors, in great osier baskets.

The Chinese emperors themselves offered to the God of the Universe, to Chang-ti, to the Tien, to the principle of all things, the first fruits of their harvest twice a year, and even of those harvests which they had sown with their own hands. This custom was kept up for upwards of forty centuries, in the midst of revolutions, and even the most horrid calamities.

Never was the religion of the emperors and of the tribunals dishonored with impostures; never was it troubled with quarrels between the priests and the empire; never was it burdened with absurd innovations, which are supported one against the other by arguments as absurd as themselves, the rage of which has at length placed the poignard in the hands of fanatics led on by the factious. Here the Chinese are particularly superior to all the nations of the universe.

Their Confucius framed neither new opinions nor new rites. He neither pretended to be an inspired man, nor a prophet. He was a magistrate, who taught the ancient laws. We sometimes say, very improperly, "the religion of Confucius"; he had no other than that of all the emperors and all the tribunals; no other than that of the first sages; he recommends nothing but virtue, preaches no mysteries; he says, in his first book, that in order to learn to govern, we should pass our whole life in correcting ourselves; in the second, he proves that God has himself graven virtue in the heart of man; he says that man is not born wicked, and that he becomes so by his own fault; the third is a collection of pure maxims, where we can meet with nothing that is mean, nor any ridiculous allegories. He had five thousand disciples, he might have put himself at the head of a powerful party; but he rather chose to instruct men, than to govern them.

The temerity we have shewn, at the extremity of the west, of judging of this eastern court, and imputing atheism to them, has been vehemently attacked in an Essay upon General History. What, in fact, must have been the rage of some amongst us, to call an empire atheistical, when almost all its laws are founded upon the knowledge of a Supreme Being, Requiter, and Avenger? The inscriptions of their temples, of which we have authentic copies, are, "To the first principle, without beginning and without end: he has done all, and governs all: he is infinitely good, infinitely just: he enlightens, he supports, and regulates all nature."

The Jesuits, who are disliked in Europe, are reproached with flattering the atheists of China. A Frenchman, named

Maigret, bishop of Conon, who did not understand a word of Chinese, was deputed by a pope, to go and try causes upon the spot; he treated Confucius as an atheist, upon these words of that great man, "Heaven has given me virtue, man cannot hurt me." The greatest of our saints never uttered a more celestial maxim. If Confucius was an atheist, so were Cato and the chancellor L'Hospital.

Let us here repeat and put calumny to the blush; that the same man who opposed Bayle, by asserting that a society of atheists was impossible, at the same time advanced, that the most ancient government upon earth was a society of atheists. We cannot be too much ashamed of our contradictions.

Let us again repeat that the literati of China, adorers of the one and only God, abandoned the people to the superstition of the Bonzes. They received the sect of Laokium, that of Fo, and several others. The magistrates conceived that the people might have different religions from that of the state, as they live upon grosser aliment; they suffered the Bonzes, and continued them. In almost every other country, those who carried on the trade of Bonzes, had the principal authority.

It is true, that the laws of China do not mention rewards and punishments after death; they did not choose to affirm what they did not know. This difference between them, and all the great polished people, is very astonishing. The doctrine of hell was useful, and the government of the Chinese never admitted it. They imagined, that an exact policy constantly exercised, would have greater effect than opinions, which might be opposed; and that the people would fear a law always present, more than one in future. We shall,

87

in the proper places, mention a people infinitely less considerable, who had nearly the same idea, or who rather had
no idea, but which was propagated by means unknown to
other men.

Let us resume here, only to add that the empire of China
subsisted with splendor, when the Chaldeans began the course
of those nineteen hundred years astronomical observations,
which were sent into Greece by Callisthenes. The Bramins
then reigned in a part of India; the Persians had their laws;
the Arabians to the south, and the Scythians to the north,
had no other habitations than tents. Egypt, which we are
now going to speak of, was a powerful kingdom.

XIX

OF EGYPT

IT EVIDENTLY appears to me that the Egyptians, as ancient as they are, could not be united into a civilized, polished, industrious body, till very long after all the people that have passed in review. The reason whereof is clear: Egypt, as far as the Delta, is inclosed by two chains of rocks, between which is the fall of the Nile, in descending from Ethiopia from south to north. From the cataracts of the Nile to its entrance, in a straight line, the distance is only 160 leagues, of 3,000 geometrical feet each; and its breadth is no more than thirteen and twenty leagues, till it washes the Delta, a low part of Egypt, which comprehends an extent of fifty leagues from east to west. On the right of the Nile are the deserts of Thebais; and on the left, the uninhabitable sands of Libya, which extend as far as the little country where the temple of Ammon was erected.

The inundations of the Nile must, in the course of ages, have removed all the columns of a land which was four months in the year under water: these stagnant waters, continually increasing, must, for a long time, have made all Egypt one continued morass. This is not the cafe upon the shores of the Tigris, the Indus, the Ganges, and other rivers, which also overflow almost every year, in the summer, when the snow melts. Their inundations are not so great,

89

and the extensive plains which surround them, enable the cultivators to completely profit of the fertility of the soil.

We should particularly observe that the plague, that inherent scourge of humanity, breaks out, at least, once in ten years in Egypt; it must have been much more destructive, when the waters of the Nile, by stagnating upon the land, added their infection to that horrid contagion; and thus the population of Egypt must have been very small for many ages.

The natural order of things seems then invincibly to demonstrate, that Egypt was one of the last inhabited lands. The Troglodytes, born upon those rocks, which are washed by the Nile, were compelled to perform labors as continual as they were difficult; to dig canals for the reception of this river; to erect cabins; and to raise them twenty-five feet above the earth. This was however, necessary before Thebes with its hundred gates, could be built; before Memphis could be erected, or the construction of pyramids could be thought of. It is very strange, that no ancient historian has made so natural a reflection.

We have already observed, that in those times, wherein Abraham's travels are placed, Egypt was a powerful king-dom: its kings had already erected some of those pyramids, which still astonish the eyes and imagination. The Arabs have written, that the greatest was erected by Saurid, several ages before Abraham; the time of building the famous Thebes, with its hundred gates, is not known. It seems that in those obscure times, great cities bore the name of the cities of God, like Babylon. But who can believe, that from each of the hundred gates of Thebes, two hundred chariots, armed in a warlike manner, and a hundred thousand warriors, issued? They would amount to twenty thousand chariots, and a million of soldiers; and if there was one soldier among every five persons, this number must make us suppose five millions of inhabitants for a single city, in a country that is not so large as Spain or France, and which, according to Diodorus Siculus, contained no more than three millions of inhabitants, and but sixty thousand soldiers for its defense. Diodorus says, (book 1st) that Egypt was so well peopled, that it formerly contained seven millions of inhabitants; and that even in his time there were three millions.

You do not give greater credit to the conquests of Sesostris, than to the million of soldiers that issued from the hundred gates of Thebes. Do you not imagine that you are reading the history of Pericles, when those who copy Herodotus tell you that the father of Sesostris, founding his hopes upon a dream, and an oracle, destined his son to conquer the world; that he brought up all the children that were born the same day as his son, in his own court, to the trade of arms; that they had no victuals allowed them till they had run the length of eight of our longest leagues; that at length Sesostris appeared with his six hundred thousand men, twenty-seven thousand warlike cars, and set out to conquer all the earth, from the Indus to the Euxine sea; and that he subjugated Mingrelia, and Georgia, then called Colchis. Herodotus does not in the least doubt that Sesostris left colonies in Colchis, because he saw tawny men with frizzled hair, who resembled Egyptians, at Colchis. I would much sooner believe, that this species of Scythians, upon the banks of the Black and Caspian seas, came to renounce

91

the Egyptians, when they ravaged, for such a length of time, Asia before the reign of Cyrus. I should believe they carried with them slaves from Egypt, that true country of slaves, whose descendants Herodotus might see, or thought he saw, in Colchis. If these Colchians had, indeed, the super-stition to be circumcised, they probably retained that custom from Egypt, as it always happened that the people of the North adopted the rites of those civilized nations whom they had conquered.

The Egyptians were never, at any known period, a for-midable people; they were never attacked by any enemy, without being conquered. The Scythians began; after the Scythians, came Nabuchodonosor, who conquered Egypt without opposition. Cyrus had nothing more to do than to send thither one of his lieutenants; when they revolted under Cambyses, one campaign was sufficient to make them submit; and this Cambyses so much despised the Egyptians, that he killed their god Apis, in their presence. Ochus reduced Egypt to a province of his kingdom. Alexander, Caesar, Augustus, and the calif Omar, conquered Egypt with equal facility. This same people of Colchis, under the name of Mammelucs, returned again to seize upon Egypt in the time of the crusades: at length Selim conquered Egypt in a single campaign, like all those who had made their appearance. There never were any other but our croises, who suffered themselves to be beat by those Egyptians, the most dastardly of mankind, as has been elsewhere observed; but this was owing to their being then governed by the Mammelucs of Colchis.

It is true that an humbled people might formerly have

been conquerors, as the Greeks and Romans testify. But we are more certain of the ancient grandeur of the Romans and Greeks, than that of Sesostris.

I do not deny that he whom we call Sesostris might have carried on a fortunate war against some Ethiopians, some Arabs, and some people of Phenicia. This was sufficient, in the language of some exaggerators, to make him the con-queror of the earth. There is no subjugated nation, who does not pretend formerly, to have subjugated others. The vain glory of ancient superiority, administers consolation for present humiliation.

Herodotus ingeniously related to the Greeks, what the Egyptians had told him; but how comes it that in speaking to him of nothing but prodigies, they gave him no intimation of the famous plagues of Egypt; of that magical battle be-tween the sorcerers of Pharaoh, and the minister of the god of the Jews; and of a whole army swallowed up in the Red Sea, under waters which rose like mountains to the right and left to let the Hebrews pass, and which, by their fall, drowned the Egyptians? This certainly was the greatest event in the history of the world. Neither Herodotus, Man-etho, or Eratosthenes, nor any of the Greeks, who were so fond of the marvellous, and who kept a regular correspond-ence with Egypt, mention these miracles, which should employ the attention of all generations. I certainly do not make this reflection to invalidate the testimony of the He-brew books, which I revere as I ought to do. I wonder only at the silence of all the Egyptians and all the Greeks. God, doubtless, was unwilling that so divine a history should be transmitted to us by any profane hand.

XX

OF THE LANGUAGE OF THE EGYPTIANS, AND THEIR SYMBOLS

THE LANGUAGE of the Egyptians had no affinity to that of the nations of Asia. You do not find among this people, the word Adeni, or Adonai, nor Bal, nor Baal, terms which signify the Lord; nor Mitra, which, with the Persians, was the Sun; nor Melch, which signified King, in Syria; nor Shak, which signifies the same thing amongst the Indians. On the contrary, you find that Pharaoh was the Egyptian name that answers to king. Ashireth (Osiris) answering to the Mirah of the Persians; and the vulgar word On, signified the Sun. The Chaldean priests called themselves Maf; those of the Egyptian Choens, as Diodorus Siculus relates. The hieroglyphics, characters, and alphabets of Egypt, which time has spared, and which we still find engraved upon the obelisks, have no relation to those of any other people.

Before men had invented hieroglyphics, they had doubtless representative signs; for in fact, what could the first men do, besides what we do, when we are in their place? Let a child be in a country ignorant of its language, and he will talk by signs; if he is not understood, he will draw upon a wall, with a piece of charcoal, the things that he wants, if he has the least sagacity.

They therefore, at first, painted in a very clumsy style,

what they wanted to communicate; and the art of drawing, doubtless, preceded that of writing. Thus it was, that the Mexicans and Peruvians wrote: they had not made any farther progress in the art: such was the method of all the first polished people. In time, they invented symbolical figures: two hands united signified peace; arts, represented war; an eye, signified the divinity; a scepter, implied royalty; and lines, which joined these figures, expressed short phrases.

The Chinese at length invented characters, to express each word of their language. But what people invented the alphabet, which in placing before our eyes the different sounds that can be articulated, facilitates the combination of all possible words by writing? who could teach men to engrave thus easily their thoughts? I shall not here repeat all the stories of the ancients upon this art, which eternizes all arts, I shall only say that many centuries were necessary to compass it.

The Choens, or priests of Egypt, continued for a long time to write in hieroglyphics, which is forbidden by the second law of the Hebrews; and when the people of Egypt had alphabetical characters, the Choens adopted different ones, which they called sacred; and in order to keep a constant barrier between them and the people, the Magi and the Bramins made use of the same kind of characters; so necessary has the art of disguise to men appeared, in order to govern them. Those Choens not only had characters peculiar to themselves, but they had still preserved the ancient language of Egypt, when time had changed the vulgar tongue.

Manetho, who is quoted by Eusebius, speaks of two columns engraved by Toth, the first Hermes, in the characters

95

of the sacred language. But who knows the period of this Hermes' existence?

The Egyptians were particularly careful in preserving their first symbols. It is curious to observe upon their monuments, a serpent biting his own tail, to represent the twelve months of the year, and each of these months expressed by animals which are not the signs of the zodiac, known to us. We again see the five days added to the twelve months, under the form of a little serpent, with five figures upon it; these are a sparrow-hawk, a man, a dog, a lion, and a stork. We see them drawn in Kirker, after the monuments preserved at Rome. Thus we find that almost every thing in antiquity was symbolical and allegorical.

XXI

OF THE MONUMENTS OF THE EGYPTIANS

IT IS certain that after the ages in which the Egyptians fertilized the soil, by the draining of the flood; after those times, when villages began to be changed into opulent cities, then the necessary arts being arrived at perfection, the ostentatious arts began to be in esteem: sovereigns were then found who employed their subjects, and some Arabs, in the neighborhood of lake Sirbon, to build them palaces and pyramid-tombs, to cut enormous stones in the quarries of Upper Egypt, and bring them afloat upon rafts, as far as Memphis; to erect upon massive columns, great flat stones, without either taste or proportion. They were acquainted with the great, but not the beautiful. They taught the first Greeks; but the Greeks were afterwards their masters in every thing, when they had built Alexandria.

It is melancholy to think, that in Caesar's wars, half of the famous library of the Ptolemies was burnt; and that the other half heated the baths of Mussulmen, when Omar subdued Egypt. We should have known at least the origin of the superstitions with which that people were infected, the chaos of their philosophy, and some of their antiquities and sciences.

They must certainly have been at peace for several ages, for their princes to have had time and leisure to raise all those prodigious buildings, the greatest part of which still subsist.

Their pyramids must have been the produce of many years and much expense; a great number of inhabitants, together with foreign slaves, must have been for a long time employed in these immense works. They were erected by despotism, vanity, servitude, and superstition; in fact, none but a despotic king could thus have constrained nature: England, for example, is more powerful than Egypt was. Could a king of England employ his people to raise such monuments?

Vanity, doubtless, had its share; it was the ambition of the ancient kings of Egypt, who should raise the finest pyramid to his father, or to himself. Servitude procured the laboring hand; and as to superstition, we know that these pyramids were tombs; we know that the Chocamatins, or Choens, of Egypt, that is to say the priests, had persuaded the people that the soul returned into its own body, at the expiration of a thousand years. They chose that the body should be a thousand years entirely free from all corruption: for which reason it was so very carefully embalmed; and to secure it from all accidents, it was inclosed in a large stone, that had no opening. The kings and great people erected tombs for themselves, in such forms as they judged would be the least exposed to the injuries of time. The preservation of their bodies surpasses all human hopes. There are now Egyptian mummies, which have been buried upwards of four thousand years. Carcasses have subsisted as long as pyramids.

This opinion of a resurrection, after ten centuries, was

98

afterwards adopted by the Greeks, who were disciples of the Egyptians, and the Romans, who were disciples of the Greeks. We find it in the sixth book of the Eneid, which is only a description of the mysteries of Isis and Ceres of Eleusinia.

> *Has omnes ubi mille rotam volvêre per annos*
> *Lethaeum ad fluvium Deus advocat agmine magno;*
> *Scilicet ut memores supera & convexa revisant.*

> But when a thousand rolling years are past,
> (So long their punishments and penance last,)
> Whole droves of minds are, by the driving god,
> Compelled to drink the deep Lethaean flood:
> In large forgetful draughts to steep the cares
> Of their past labors, and their irksome years.

It was afterwards introduced amongst the Christians, who established the reign of a thousand years; the sect of the Millenarians has handed it down to our time. Thus have many opinions passed all over the world. This is sufficient to point out the design of erecting those pyramids. We shall not repeat what has been said upon their architecture and dimensions; I examine only the history of the human under-standing.

XXII

OF THE EGYPTIAN RITES, AND CIRCUMCISION

IN THE first place, did the Egyptians acknowledge one supreme God? If this question had been proposed to the commonalty of that people themselves, they would not have known what to reply: if to the young students in Egyptian theology, they would have harangued for a long time, without understanding themselves: if to any one of the sages consulted by Pythagoras, Plato, or Plutarch, he would ingeniously have replied, that he adored only one God, which answer would be founded upon the ancient inscription of the statue of Isis, "I am what is"; and this other, "I am all that has been and will be; no mortal can raise my veil." He would have pointed out the globe, placed upon the temple-gate of Memphis, which represented the unity of the divine nature, under the word *knef*. The most sacred name amongst the Egyptians, was that which the Hebrews adopted, ϒ *ha ho*. It is variously pronounced; but Clement of Alexandria assures us, in his Stromates, that those who entered into the temple of Serapis, were obliged to wear the inscription of the name *I ha ho*, or *I ha hou*, which signified the God eternal. The Arabians have retained only the syllable *hou*, afterwards adopted by the Turks, who pronounce it with still greater respect than the word *allah;* for they use *allah* in conversation, and they never utter *hou*, but when at prayer. Let us observe here (en passant) that when the Turkish ambassador, Said Effendi, saw the representation of the *Bourgeois gentilhomme* (or Tradesman turned Gentleman) and that ridiculous ceremony in which he is made a Turk, and hearing the sacred word *hou* pronounced with derision and extravagant gestures, he looked upon this derision as the most abominable profanation.

But to resume. The Egyptian priests feed a sacred ox, a sacred dog, and a sacred crocodile, it is very true; and the Romans had also their sacred geese: they had gods of every kind, and the devotees had, among their household deities, the god of the open-chair, *Deum stercutium,* and the god *Pet, Deum crepitum;* but did they less acknowledge the *Deum optimum maximum,* the master of gods and men? Which is the country that has not abounded with superstitious bigots, and a small number of reasonable people?

What should be particularly observed with respect to Egypt and all other nations, is, that they never had any invariable opinions, any more than laws, that were always uniform, notwithstanding the attachment which men have to their ancient customs. There is nothing immutable but geometry, all things else undergo incessant variation.

The learned dispute, and will dispute. One asserts that the ancient people were all idolaters, another denies it; one says that they adored only one God, without an image; another says that they adored several gods, in several images. They are all right; nothing more is requisite than to distinguish the times and men which have changed; there never was any agreement. When the Ptolemies, and the principal

101

priests, made a joke of Apis's bull, the people prostrated themselves before it.

Juvenal says, that the Egyptians adored onions; but we do not find it in any history. There is a great deal of difference between a sacred onion, and an onion that is a god: everything is not adored that is placed, that is consecrated, upon the altar. We read in Cicero, that those men who have drained every kind of superstition, have not yet arrived at that of eating their gods; and that this is the only absurdity they are deficient in.

Is circumcision derived from the Egyptians, the Arabians, or the Ethiopians? I am ignorant. Let those who know speak. All I know is, that the priests of antiquity imprinted upon their bodies marks of their consecration, as the Roman soldiers were afterwards marked with a hot iron. There the sacrificing priests slashed the bodies, as did afterwards the priests of Bellona: here they made themselves eunuchs, in imitation of the priests of Cybele.

It was not in order to preserve health, that the Ethiopians, the Arabians, and the Egyptians, circumcised themselves. It is said, that their prepuce was too long; but if an opinion may be formed of a nation by an individual, I have seen a young Ethiopian, who, being born out of his country, was not circumcised; and I can aver that his prepuce was precisely the same as ours.

I do not know what nation first thought proper to make a procession of the Kteis and the Phallum, that is to say, a representation of the distinctive signs of male and female animals; a ceremony which would be now indecent, but which was formerly sacred. This custom prevailed amongst

102

the Egyptians; first fruits were offered to the gods, the most precious things were immolated to them. It seemed natural and just, that the priests should offer up a small part of the organ of generation, to those by whom every thing was engendered. The Ethiopians and Arabians also circumcised their daughters, by cutting away a very small part of the nymphae; which proves that neither health nor cleanliness could be the reason of this ceremony, for certainly a girl uncircumcised may be as clean as one that is circumcised.

When the priests of Egypt had consecrated this opera' tion, their initiated also underwent it; but, in time, this mark of distinction was given up to the priests alone. We do not find that any one of the Ptolemies had been circum' cised; and the other Romans never disgraced the Egyptians with the name of Apella, which they gave to the Jews. The Jews had adopted circumcision from the Egyptians, with part of their ceremonies. They have always retained it, as well as the Arabians and the Ethiopians; the Turks have submitted to it, though it is not ordered in the Alcoran. It is only ancient usage, which was introduced by superstition, and which has been preserved by custom.

XXIII

OF THE MYSTERIES OF THE EGYPTIANS

I AM far from knowing what nation first invented these mysteries, which have gained so much credit from the Euphrates to the Tiber. The Egyptians make no mention of the author of the mysteries of Isis. Those established in Persia are attributed to Zoroaster, those of Greece to Cadmus and Inachus, those of Thrace to Orpheus, and those of Crete to Minos. It is certain that all these mysteries intimate a future state; for Celsus says to the Christians, "You boast of believing in eternal punishments, and do not all the ministers of mysteries declare them to the initiated?"

The Greeks, who borrowed so many things from the Egyptians; their Tartharoth, of which they made the Tartarus; the lake, of which they made the Acheron; the waterman Charon, of whom they made the ferryman of the dead, framed their famous mysteries of Eleusinia only upon the model of those of Isis. But no one can affirm that the mysteries of Zoroaster did not precede those of the Egyptians: they are both of the greatest antiquity, and all the Greek and Latin authors, who have made mention of them, agree that the unity of God, the immortality of the soul, rewards and punishments after death, were pronounced in these sacred ceremonies.

It is very probable that the Egyptians, having once established these mysteries, preserved their rites; for notwith-standing their extreme levity, they were invariable in their superstition. The prayer which we meet with in Apuleius, when Lucius is initiated into the mysteries of Isis, must have been the ancient prayer: "The celestial powers serve thee, the infernal regions are in submission to thee, the universe turns round in thine hand, thy feet stamp upon Tartarus, the stars reply to thy voice, the seasons return at thy order, the elements obey thee, etc."

Can there be a stronger evidence of the unity of one only God, acknowledged by the Egyptians, in the midst of all their contemptible superstitions?

XXIV

OF THE GREEKS; OF THEIR ANCIENT DELUGES; OF THEIR ALPHABET, AND THEIR GENIUS

GREECE IS a small hilly country, intersected by the sea, of much the same extent as Great Britain. Everything in this country testifies the physical revolutions it has under-gone. The islands which surround it sufficiently show, by the continued shoals near their shores, by the shallowness of the sea, by the herbs and roots which grow under the water, that they were detached from the continent. The gulfs of Eubius, Calcis, Argos, Corinth, Actium, and Mes-sina, demonstrate that the sea has made passages through the earth. The sea-shell beds, with which are covered those mountains that surround the famous vale of Tempe, are ocular proofs of an ancient inundation: and the deluges of Ogiges and Deucalion, which have produced so many fables, are historically true. This may probably be the reason why the Greeks are so new a people. These great revolutions sunk them once more in barbarity, at the time that the nations of Asia and Egypt were flourishing.

I shall leave to men more learned than myself, the trouble of proving that the three children of Noah, who were the only inhabitants of the globe, divided the whole of it amongst them; that they separated from each other two or three thou-sand leagues, laying every where the foundation of powerful empires; and that Javan, his grandson, peopled all Greece, in passing through Italy; that from thence the Greeks derived the name of Ionians, Ion having detached colonies upon the coasts of Asia Minor; that Ion plainly appears to be Javan, by changing the S into *Sa,* and the *on* into *van.* Such tales are told to children, and children do not believe them:

Nec pueri credunt nisi qui nondum aere lavantur.

The deluge of Ogiges is usually placed about twelve hundred years before the first olympiad: the first who speaks of it is Acesitas, quoted by Eusebius, in his Evangelical Preparation, and by George le Sincelle. Greece, it is said, remained a desert two hundred years after the sea had made this eruption into the country. It is, nevertheless, asserted, that a government was at the same time established in Siciones and in Argos; the names of the first magistrates of these little provinces are even mentioned, and they are called Basiloi, which answers to princes. But let us not lose time in penetrating these useless obscurities.

There was another inundation in the time of Deucalion, the son of Prometheus. The fable adds that there remained no other inhabitants than Deucalion and Pyrrha, who made fresh men, by throwing stones behind them, through their legs. The world is stocked with men faster than a warren is with rabbits.

If very judicious men, like Petau the Jesuit, is to be believed, a single son of Noah produced a race, which, at the end of twenty-eight years, amounted to six hundred and twenty-three thousand millions, six hundred and twelve millions of men. The calculation is a little high. We are so un-happy at present, that in twenty-six marriages, there are usually but four which produce children that become fathers. This calculation is formed upon the accounts of the registers of the greatest cities. Of a thousand children that are born the same year, there are scarce six hundred remaining at the end of twenty years. Let us suspect the veracity of Petau, and such, who like him, create children with the stroke of a pen, as well as those who relate that Deucalion and Pyrrha peopled Greece by throwing stones.

Greece, we know, was the country of fables, and almost every fable was the origin of a doctrine, of a temple, and a public feast. By what excess of madness, by what absurd obstinacy, have so many compilers endeavored to prove, in so many enormous volumes, that a public feast, established in commemoration of an event, is a demonstration of the truth of that event? What, because young Bacchus is cele-brated in a temple issuing from Jupiter's thigh, Jupiter really had concealed Bacchus in his thigh? What, Cadmus and his wife were changed into serpents, in Boeotia, because the Boeotians commemorated such an event in their ceremonies! Did the temples of Castor and Pollux, at Rome, demon-strate that those gods descended upon earth, in favor of the Romans?

Much rather assure yourself, when you see an ancient feast, or an antique temple, that they are the works of error. This error gains credit at the end of two or three centuries; it afterwards becomes sacred, and temples are erected to chimeras.

On the contrary, in historical times, the most noble truths

have but few sectaries; the greatest men die without honor. The Themistocleses, the Cimons, the Miltiadeses, the Aristideses, the Phocions, are persecuted; whilst Perseus, Bacchus, and other fanatical personages, have temples.

Credit may be given to a people with regard to what they say of themselves to their own disadvantage, when these accounts are attended with probability, and are no way contradictory to the common order of nature.

The Athenians, who were dispersed in a very barren land, inform us themselves, that an Eyyptian, named Cyclops, who was driven out of his country, gave them their first institutions. This appears surprising, because the Egyptians were not navigators; but it might have happened that the Phoenicians, who travelled throughout all nations, carried Cyclops into Attica. It is very certain, that the Greeks did not adopt the Egyptian letters, which heirs no way resemble. The Phoenicians carried them their first alphabet, which then consisted of only sixteen characters, and are evidently the same. The Phoenicians afterwards added eight letters, which the Greeks still retain.

I look upon an alphabet as an incontestible monument of the country from whence a nation derived its first knowledge. It appears very probable, again, that these Phoenicians discovered the silver mines, which were in Attica, as they worked those of Spain. Merchants were the first preceptors of these same Greeks, who afterwards instructed all other nations.

These people, all barbarous as they were in the time of Ogiges, seem to have been born with organs more favorable to the fine arts, than any other people. They had something in their nature more cunning and subtle: their language evinces it; for even before they knew how to write, we find that they had a more harmonious mixture of soft consonants and vowels in their language, than any other people of Asia were ever acquainted with.

The name of Knath, which signifies the Phoenicians, according to Sanchoniatho, is certainly not so harmonious as that of Hellenos or Graios. Argos, Athens, Lacedemon, and Olympus, sound better to the ear than the city of Reheboth. Sophia, wisdom, is softer than Shochemath in Syriac and Basileus in Hebrew. Roy sounds better than Melk or Shack. Compare the names of Agamemnon, Diomede, Idomeneus, with those of Mardokempad, Simordak, Sohasduch, Niricassolahssar. Joseph himself, in his book against Appion, acknowledges that the Greeks could not pronounce the barbarous name of Jerusalem, because the Jews pronounced it Hershalaïm: this word grated the throat of an Athenian; and it was changed by the Greeks from Hershalaïm to Jerusalem.

The Greeks transformed all the harsh Syriac, Persian, and Egyptian names. Of Coresh they made Cyrus; of Isheth and Oshireth, they made Isis and Osiris; of Moph, they made Memphis, and at length brought the Barbarians to accustom themselves to their pronunciation; so that in the time of the Ptolemies, the Egyptian cities and gods had no other than Grecian names.

The Indus and Ganges had their names from the Greeks. The Ganges, in the Bramins' language, was called Sannoubi, and the Indus Sombadipo. Such are the ancient names that we find in the Vedam.

The Greeks, in extending themselves upon the coasts of Asia Minor, carried with them their harmony. Their Homer was probably born at Smyrna.

Fine architecture, perfect sculpture, painting, and good music, real poetry, real eloquence, the method of writing good history, and, in a word, philosophy, though unfashioned and obscure; all these things were handed down to other nations by the Greeks. The last comers surpassed their masters in everything.

Egypt had never any fine statues by Grecian hands. Ancient Balbec in Syria, ancient Palmyra in Arabia, had not those regular magnificent palaces and temples, till the sovereigns of those countries called in Grecian artists. We find nothing but the remains of barbarism, as has been in another place observed, in the ruins of Persepolis, built by the Persians; and the monuments of Balbec and Palmyra are still, under their ruins, master-pieces of architecture.

XXV

OF THE GREEK LEGISLATORS, OF MINOS AND ORPHEUS, AND OF THE IMMORTALITY OF THE SOUL

HOW MANY compilers repeat the battles of Marathon and Salaminia? These are great exploits that are very well known: others are incessantly telling us that a proud son of Noah, named Settim, was king of Macedon, because in the first book of Maccabees, it is said that Alexander went out of the country of Kittim. Other objects shall engage my attention.

Minos lied about the time in which ye place Moses; and this has given the learned Huet, bishop of Avranche, some false grounds to maintain that Minos, born in Crete, and Moses, born upon the confines of Egypt, were the same person; a system which, as absurd as it is, has found some partisans.

This is not a Grecian fable; Minos was doubtless a legislative king. The famous marbles of Paros, those most precious monuments of antiquity (and for which we are indebted to the English) fix his birth four hundred and eighty-two years before our vulgar era. Homer, in his Odyssey, calls him "The wife confident of God." Flavian Josephus does not hesitate saying that he received his laws from a god. This is a little strange in a Jew, who, it should seem, ought

112

to allow no other god than his own, unless he thought like the Romans his masters, and like all the first people of antiquity, who allowed the existence of all the gods of other nations.

It is certain that Minos was a very rigid legislator, as it was supposed that he should judge the departed souls in the infernal regions; it is evident that the belief of a future state generally prevailed, at that time, in a considerable part of Asia and Europe.

Orpheus is as real a personage as Minos: it is true that the marbles of Paros do not mention him; this probably was because he was not born in Greece, properly so called, but in Thrace. Some have doubted the existence of the first Orpheus, upon a passage of Cicero, in his excellent book upon the Nature of the Gods. Cotta, one of the interlocutors, avers that Aristotle did not believe that this Orpheus had been amongst the Greeks; but Aristotle makes no mention of him in those works of his which are handed down to us. Besides, the opinion of Cotta does not coincide with that of Cicero. A hundred ancient writers mention Orpheus. The mysteries which bear his name testify his existence. Pausanias, who was the most exact writer amongst the Greeks, says, that his verses were sung in religious ceremonies, in preference to those of Homer, who did not live till a great while afterwards. We know very well he did not descend into hell; but even this fable proves that the infernal regions were a point of the theology of those remote times.

The vague opinion of the permanence of the soul after death, an aerial soul, a shadow of the body, manes, a light breeze, an unknown, incomprehensible soul, but yet exciting,

113

and the belief of rewards and punishments in a future state, were adopted throughout Greece, in the islands, in Asia, and in Egypt.

The Jews were the only people who appeared entirely ignorant of this mystery; the book of their laws does not make the least mention of it: we there meet with nothing but temporary rewards and punishments. In Exodus, we read, "Honor thy father and thy mother, that Adonai may prolong thy days upon earth:" in the book of Zend (part II) we find, "Honor father and mother, in order to deserve heaven."

Bishop Warburton, who has demonstrated, that the Pentateuch makes no mention of the immortality of the soul, supposes that this dogma was not necessary in theocracy. Arnaud, in his Apology of Port Royal, expresses himself thus: "It is the summit of ignorance to doubt of this truth, which is the most prevalent, and which is attested by all the fathers, that the promises made in the Old Testament are only temporary and terrestrial, and that the Jews adored God only for carnal advantages."

It has been objected, that if the Persians, the Arabians, the Syrians, the Indians, the Egyptians, and the Greeks, believed in the immortality of the soul, a future life, eternal rewards and punishments, the Hebrews might also believe them: that if all the legislators of antiquity have established wife laws upon this foundation, Moses might also have done the same: that if he was ignorant of those useful dogmas, he was unworthy of leading a nation: that if he knew them and concealed them, he was still more unworthy.

To these arguments, it is answered, that God, whose organ was Moses, deigned to level himself to the meanness of the Jews' capacity; I shall not engage in this thorny question, and constantly respecting every thing that is divine, I shall continue examining the history of men.

XXVI

OF THE SECTS AMONGST THE GREEKS

IT APPEARS that amongst the Egyptians, amongst the Persians, amongst the Chaldeans, and amongst the Indians, there was but one sect of philosophy. The priests of these nations were all of a particular race; what was called wisdom belonged only to this race. Their sacred tongue, unknown to the people, confined all science to them. But in Greece, which was more free and happy, the avenues to reason were open to every one: all people gave vent to their ideas; and, by this means, the Greeks became the most ingenious people upon earth. And thus, in our time, the English nation is become the most enlightened, because men may think with impunity amongst them.

The Stoics adopted one universal soul of the world, wherein all the souls of living creatures were replunged. The Epicureans denied there was a soul, and were acquainted with nothing but physical principles. They maintained that the gods did not concern themselves with worldly affairs; and the Epicureans were left in peace, as they had left the gods.

The schools re-echoed from the time of Thales to the time of Plato and Aristotle, with philosophical disputes; which at once disclose the wisdom and folly of the human mind, its grandeur and weakness. They argued, almost con-

116

stantly, without understanding one another, as we have done since the thirteenth century, when we began to reason.

Plato's reputation does not astonish me; all philosophers were unintelligible; they were as much so as other people, and expressed themselves with greater eloquence. But what success would Plato have, if he were to appear now in the company of sensible men, and if he repeated to them those fine words which are in his Timaeus?

"Of divisible and indivisible substance, God composed a third kind of substance, between both, partaking of the nature of the *same and the other;* then taking these three natures together, he mixed them all into one form, and forced the nature of the soul to mix with the nature of *the same;* and having mixed them with the substance, and of these three having made an agent, he divided it into proper portions; each of these portions was mixed with the same and the other; and of the substance, he made his division."

He afterwards explains with equal perspicuity, the quaternity of Pythagoras. It must be acknowledged, that reasonable men who had lately read Locke upon the Human Understanding, would desire Plato to go to his school.

These extravagances of the good Plato do not prevent our frequently meeting with beautiful ideas in his work. The Greeks had so much sense, that they trifled with it. But what does them great honor is, that none of their governments confined men's thoughts: Socrates may, perhaps, be excepted, as his opinions cost him his life: but he was less the victim of his opinions than of a violent party, who formed themselves against him. The Athenians, indeed, made him drink gall; but we also know how much they repented of it:

117

we know, that they punished his accusers, and that they erected a temple to him whom they had condemned. Athens did not only allow entire liberty to philosophy, but to all kinds of religion. It received all foreign gods, and it had even an altar dedicated to the unknown gods.

It is incontestable, that the Greeks acknowledged a supreme God, as well as all the nations we have mentioned. Their Zeus, their Jupiter, was the master of gods and men. This opinion never changed since Orpheus: we meet with it a hundred times in Homer: all the other gods are subordinate. They may be compared to the Peris of the Persians, and to the genii of the oriental nations. All philosophers, except the Stratonicians and the Epicureans, acknowledged the architect of the world, the Demiourgoi.

We need not fear building too much upon this great historical truth, that the dawn of human reason adored some power which was judged to be superior to common power, whether the sun, the moon, or the stars; that human reason being cultivated, notwithstanding all its errors, adored a God, supreme master of the elements and the other gods; and that all the polished people from the Indus to the extremities of Europe, believed, in general, in a future state; though many sects of philosophers were of a different opinion.

XXVII

OF ZALEUCUS, AND SOME OTHER LEGISLATORS

I DARE here defy all moralists and legislators, and I ask them all, if they ever delivered anything finer, or more use' ful, than the exordium of the laws of Zaleucus, who lived before Pythagoras, and who was the first magistrate of the Locrians?

"Every citizen should be persuaded of the existence of the divinity. It is only necessary to observe the order and harmony of the universe, to be convinced that accident could not have formed it. We should subdue the soul, purify it, and cleanse it from all evil; in the persuasion that God can' not be well served by those of a perverse disposition; and that he does not resemble those wretched mortals, who let themselves be wrought upon by magnificent ceremonies and sumptuous offerings. Virtue alone, and a constant disposition of doing good, can please him. Let us then endeavor to be just in our principles and practice; we shall thereby become dear to the divinity. Every one should dread more what leads to ignominy, than what leads to poverty. He should be looked upon as the best citizen, who gives up his fortune for justice; but those whose violent passions lead them to evil, men, women, citizens, common inhabitants, should be cautioned to remember the gods, and to think often of the severe judgments which they exercise against the wicked;

119

let them have the hour of their death before their eyes, the fatal hour which awaits us all, the hour when the remembrance of faults brings on remorse, and the vain regret of not having let all our actions be swayed by equity.

"Everyone should therefore conduct himself, as if this moment was the last of his life; but if an evil genius prompts him to crimes, let him fly to the foot of the altar, and implore heaven to drive from him the ill-disposed genius; let him particularly throw himself into the arms of worthy people, whose counsels will bring him back to virtue, by representing to him God's goodness and his vengeance."

No; there is nothing in all antiquity that should obtain a preference to this simple, but sublime moral, dictated by reason and virtue, stripped of enthusiasm and of those gigantic figures, which good sense disowns.

Charondas, a disciple of Zaleucus, explained himself in the same manner. The Platos, Ciceros, and divine Antoniuses, have never since held any other language. Thus does Julian, who had the misfortune to give up the Christian religion, but who did so much honor to that of nature, explain himself; that Julian, who was the scandal of our church, and the glory of the Roman empire.

"The ignorant," says he, "should be instructed, and not punished; they should be pitied, and not hated; the duty of an emperor is to imitate God; to imitate him is to have the fewest wants, and to do him all the good that is possible."

Let those who insult antiquity, learn to be acquainted with it; let them not confound wife legislators with fabulists; let them know how to distinguish between the laws of the wisest magistrates, and the ridiculous customs of the people;

120

let them not say that superstitious ceremonies were invented, that false oracles and false prodigies were without number; and that all the magistrates of Greece and Rome who tolerated them, were blindly imposed upon as well as impostors: this would be like saying there are bonzes in China who abuse the populace, and that therefore the wife of Confucius was a wretched impostor.

Men should, in so enlightened an age as this, blush at those declamations, which ignorance has so often promulgated against sages, who should be imitated, and not calumniated. Do we not know that in every country the vulgar are imbecile, superstitious, and insensible? Have there not been convulsionaries in the country of the chancellor de L'Hôpital, of Charon, Montagne, de la Motte, la Voyer, Descartes, Bayle, Fontenelle, and Montesquieu? Are there not Methodists, Moravians, Millenarians, and fanatics of every kind, in that country which was so fortunate as to give birth to the chancellor Bacon, to those immortal geniuses Newton and Locke, and to a multitude of great men?

XXVIII

OF BACCHUS

EXCEPT THOSE fables that are plainly allegorical, like that of the Muses, of Venus, of the Graces, of Love, of Zephyrus, and Flora, and a few more of this kind; all the rest are a jumble of tales that can have no other merit than that of having furnished Ovid and Quinaut with good verses, and of having exercised the pencils of our best painters: but there is one that seems to deserve the attention of those who admire researches into antiquity; this is the fable of Bacchus.

Was this Bacchus, or Back, or Backos, or Dionysos, son of God, a real personage? Many nations mention him as well as Hercules; so many different Herculeses and Bac-chuses have been celebrated, that it may be supposed that there was, in fact, one Bacchus, as well as one Hercules.

It is certain, that in Egypt, Asia, and Greece, Bacchus as well as Hercules was acknowledged for a demi-god; that their feasts were celebrated; that miracles were attributed to them; and that mysteries were instituted in the name of Bacchus before the Jewish books were known.

We know that the Jews did not communicate their books to foreigners, till the time of Ptolomy Philadelphus, about two hundred and thirty years before our era. Now, before that time, the East and West re-echoed with the orgies of

Bacchus. The verses that are attributed to the ancient Orpheus celebrated the conquests and good actions of this
supposed demi-god. His history is so ancient, that the fathers
of the church suppose Bacchus to have been Noah, because
Bacchus and Noah are both reckoned to have cultivated the
vine.

Herodotus in relating the ancient opinions says, that
Bacchus was an Egyptian, brought up in Arabia Felix. The
Orphic verses say, that he was saved from the waters in a
small box, which was called Misem, in remembrance of this
adventure; that he was instructed in the secrets of the gods;
that he had a wand, which he changed into a serpent at
will; that he passed the Red Sea dry-footed, as Hercules did
afterwards the straits of Callipolis and Abila in his jug-
gler's box; that when he went into India, he and his army
enjoyed the sun-shine during the night; that he touched with
his enchanting wand, the waters of the rivers Orontes and
Hydaspes; and that these waters separated, and left him a
free passage. It is even said, that he stopped the course of
the sun and moon. He wrote his laws upon two stone tables.
He was anciently represented with horns, or rays, which
issued from his head.

After this, it is not surprising, that several learned men,
and particularly Bochart, and Huet latterly, should suppose
that Bacchus was a copy of Moses and Joshua. Everything
concurs to favor the resemblance; for Bacchus was, amongst
the Egyptians, called Arsaph, and amongst the names which
the fathers have given to Moses, we find that of Osasirph.

Between these two histories, which appear similar in
so many respects, it is not to be doubted that the history

of Moses is the real one, and that of Bacchus only the fable. But it appears that this fable was known to several nations long before the history of Moses had reached them. No Greek author before Longinus, who lived under the emperor Aurelian, quoted Moses; and all had celebrated Bacchus.

It appears incontestable, that the Greeks could not take the idea of Bacchus from the book of the Jewish laws, which they did not understand, and of which they had not the least knowledge; a book, that was moreover so scarce, even amongst the Jews, that in the reign of King Josias, there was only one copy to be found; a book that was almost entirely lost during the slavery of the Jews, who were transported into Chaldea, and the other parts of Asia; a book that was afterwards restored by Esdras in the flourishing times of Athens, and the other Grecian republics; times when the mysteries of Bacchus were already instituted.

God then allowed that the spirit of untruth should reveal the absurdities of the life of Bacchus to a hundred nations, before the spirit of truth divulged the life of Moses to any other people but the Jews.

The learned bishop of Avranche, struck with this sur-prising semblance, did not hesitate pronouncing, that Moses was not only Bacchus, but the Thaut, the Osiris of the Egyptians. He even adds, to remove any contradiction, that Moses was also their Typhon,* that is to say, that he was at the same time, the good and bad principle, the protector and the enemy, the God and Devil of the Egyptians.

Moses, according to this learned man, is the same as Zoroaster. He is Esculapius, Amphion, Apollo, Faunus,

* Proposition 4. p. 79, and 87.

Janus, Perseus, Romulus, Vertumnus, and, at last, Adonis and Priapus. The proof of his being Adonis, is that Virgil says,

Et formosus oves ad flumina pavit Adonis,

And the sheep were guarded by the fair Adonis.

Now Moses watched the sheep towards Arabia. The proof of his being Priapus is still better. Priapus was some-times represented with an ass, and the Jews were supposed to adore an ass. Huet adds, to complete the confirmation, that Moses's rod might very well be compared to the scepter of Priapus:

Sceptrum Priapo tribuitur, virga Masi.

This is what he calls demonstration. It is not, indeed, very geometrical. There is reason to believe that he blushed at it in the latter part of his life; and that he recollected his demonstration, when he wrote his Treatise upon the Weak-ness of the Human Mind and of the Uncertainty of its Knowledge.

XXIX

OF THE METAMORPHOSES AMONGST THE GREEKS, COLLECTED BY OVID

THE OPINION of the transmigration of souls naturally leads to metamorphoses, as we have already seen. Every idea that strikes the imagination, and amuses it, presently spreads throughout the world. As soon as you have persuaded me, that my soul can enter into the body of a horse, it will not be difficult for you to make me believe, that my body may be also changed into a horse.

The metamorphoses collected by Ovid, which we have already slightly touched upon, should, in no respect, astonish a Pythagorian, a Bramin, a Chaldean, or an Egyptian. The gods were changed into animals in ancient Egypt. Derceto was become a fish in Syria; Semiramis was changed into a dove in Babylon. The Jews write in much more early times, that Nabuchodonosor was changed into a bull, without including Lot's wife, who was transformed into a pillar of salt. Are not the apparitions of gods and genii in human shape real though transitory metamorphoses?

A god cannot well commune with us, unless he be metamorphosed into man. It is true that Jupiter took upon him the figure of a beautiful swan to enjoy Leda. But these cases are seldom met with; and in all religions the divinity takes upon him a human shape, when he comes to give orders.

It would be difficult to understand the voice of gods, if they appeared in the shape of bears or crocodiles.

In fine, the gods metamorphosed themselves in almost every place; and as soon as we were instructed in the secrets of magic, we metamorphosed ourselves. Many credible people transformed themselves into wolves; and the word *wolf-man* is still a proof amongst us of this metamorphosis.

What gives weight to the belief of all these prodigies and transmutations, is that no formal proof can be given of their impossibility. There is no argument to be opposed, if a person should aver that a god came yesterday to my house in the figure of a handsome young man, and my daughter will be brought to bed in nine months of a beautiful child that the God had deigned to confer upon her. My brother, who was so daring as to doubt the fact, was turned into a wolf: he actually went into the woods and howled. If the girl is really brought to bed, if the man who is changed into a wolf affirms that he has actually undergone this metamorphosis, you cannot demonstrate that the thing is not true. The only resource left you is to summon before a judge the young man, who counterfeited a god, and impregnated the young lady; and to watch the uncle, the *wolf-man,* and get witnesses of the imposture: but the family will not expose themselves to this examination; they will maintain with the priests of the Canton, that you are a profane ignorant man; they will show you that since a caterpillar can be changed into a butterfly, a man with equal facility may be changed into a beast; and, if you dispute, you will be impeached at the inquisition of the country, as an impious wretch, who neither believes in *men-wolves,* nor in gods, who get girls with child.

127

XXX

OF IDOLATRY

AFTER HAVING read all that has been written upon idolatry, there is nothing that communicates a precise idea of it. It seems that Locke was the first who taught men to define the words they uttered, and not talk at random. The term that answers to idolatry is not to be found in any ancient language; it is an expression of the Greeks of the last ages, which was never in use before the second century of our era. It signifies the adoration of images; it is a term of reproach, an injurious word; no people ever took upon themselves the title of idolaters; no government ever ordained that the people should adore an image, as the supreme God of nature. The ancient Chaldeans, the ancient Arabians, the ancient Persians, had, for a long time, neither images nor temples. How could those who venerated in the sun, the stars, and fire, the emblems of the divinity, be called idolaters? they revered what they saw. But surely revering the sun and the stars is not adoring a moulded image, made by a workman; this is following an erroneous doctrine, but this is not idolatry.

Suppose that the Egyptians really adored the dog Anubis, and the bull Apis: that they were fools enough to consider them not as animals consecrated to the divinity, and as an emblem of the good, which their Isheth and their Isis, did unto man, but really believed that a celestial ray animated the consecrated ox and dog; it is evident this was not adoring a statue. A beast is not an idol.

Men had, doubtless, objects of devotion before they had sculptors; and it is clear that those men who were so ancient could not be called idolaters. It remains then to know, if those who afterwards placed statues in the temples, and who made these statues be revered, called themselves adorers of statues, and their people the adorers of statues. This certainly is not to be found in any monument of antiquity.

But without taking upon themselves the title of idolaters, were they really so in fact? Was it ordained that they should believe that the brazen statue, which represented the fantastical figures of Bel and Babylon, was the master, the God, the creator of the world? was the figure of Jupiter, Jupiter himself? is not this (if it be allowed to compare the customs of our holy religion with the customs of antiquity) like saying that we adore the figure of the eternal father with a long beard, the figure of a woman and a child, the figure of a dove? these are emblematical ornaments in our temples. We adore them so little, that as soon as these statues, when of wood, begin to rot, we turn them into fuel: they are nothing more than advertisements dedicated to the eyes and the imagination. The Turks, and those of the reformed church, think that the Catholics are idolaters; but the Catholics incessantly protest against this injurious accusation.

It is impossible really to adore a statue, or to believe that any statue can be the supreme God. There was but one Jupiter, but there are a thousand statues of him. Now, this Jupiter, who was thought to dart his lightning, was sup-

129

posed to inhabit the clouds, or mount Olympus, or the planet which bears his name. His emblems did not dart lightning, and were neither in a planet, in the clouds, nor upon mount Olympus. All prayers were dedicated to the immortal Gods, and assuredly the statues were not immortal.

Cheats, no doubt, made it be believed, and the superstitious did believe, that statues had spoken. How often have our ignorant people had the same credulity? But these absurdities were never, amongst any people, the religion of the state. Some stupid old woman may not have distinguished the statue from the god; this is no reason for maintaining that the government thought like this old woman. The magistrates were willing that the representation of the gods they adored should be revered, and that the attention of the people should be fixed by these visible signs. This is precisely the same thing that is done by half Europe. We have figures that represent God the father, under the form of an old man, and we know very well that God is not an old man. We have the images of several saints, whom we revere, and we know very well that these saints are not God the Father.

In the same manner, if I may be allowed to say it, the ancients did not confound the demi-gods, the gods, and the master of the gods. If the ancients were idolaters for having statues in their temples, one half of Christendom are also idolaters; and, if they are not, the ancient nations were not so either.

In a word, there is not in all antiquity a single poet, a single philosopher, a single man of any rank, who has said that stone, marble, brass, or wood, should be adored. There are innumerable testimonies to the contrary; idolatrous na tions are then like sorcerers; they are spoken of, but they never existed.

A commentator has concluded that the statue of Priapus was really adored, because Horace, in making this scarecrow speak, puts these words into his mouth, "I was formerly a log; the workman, doubtful whether he should make a god or a joint-stool, resolved to make a god of it, etc." The commentator quotes the prophet Baruch, to prove, that in the time of Horace, the figure of Priapus was looked upon as a real divinity. He does not perceive that Horace makes a joke both of the pretended god and the statue. It might happen that one of his servants, observing this enormous figure, thought that there was something divine in it; but surely all those wooden Priapuses, with which the gardens were filled to scare birds, were not looked upon as the creators of the world.

It is said that Moses, notwithstanding the divine law which forbade the making of the representation of men or animals, erected a brazen serpent, which was an imitation of the silver serpent carried by the Egyptian priests in procession; but though this serpent was made to cure the bites of real serpents, it was not, however, adored. Solomon placed two cherubims in the temple; but these cherubims were not looked upon as gods. If then, in the temple of the Jews, and in our temples, statues have been respected without idolatry, why should other nations be so much reproached? We should either absolve them, or they should accuse us.

XXXI

OF ORACLES

IT IS evident we cannot be acquainted with futurity, because we cannot be acquainted with what does not exist; but
it is also clear that conjectures may be formed of an event.

You see a numerous and well disciplined army, conducted by a skilful chief, advancing in an advantageous
place, against an imprudent captain, followed by only a
few troops, badly armed, badly posted, and half of whom
you know to be traitors, you foretell that this captain will
be defeated.

You have observed that a young man and a young woman
are desperately fond of each other; you saw each of them
come from their own home; you announce that in a short
time this girl will be with child; you cannot be much mistaken.
All predictions are reduced to the calculation of probabilities:
there is therefore no nation in which some predictions have
not been made that have come to pass. The most celebrated
and best attested, is that which the traitor Flavian Josephus
made to Vespasian and Titus his son, the conquerors of the
Jews. He saw Vespasian and Titus adored by the Roman
armies in the East, and Nero detested by the whole empire.
He had the audacity, in order to obtain the good graces
of Vespasian, to predict to him, in the name of the God of
the Jews,* that he and his son would become emperors.

* Joseph. Book iii. ch. 28.

132

They, in effect, were so; but it is evident that Josephus ran no risque. If the day of Vespasian's overthrow had come, he would not have been in a situation to punish Josephus: if he obtained the imperial throne, he must recompense his prophet; and till such time as he reigned, he was in hopes of doing it. Vespasian informed this Josephus, that if he were a prophet, he should have foretold him the loss of Jotapat, which he had ineffectually defended against the Roman army: Josephus replied, that he had in fact foretold it, which was not very surprising; what commander, who sustains a siege in a small place against a numerous army, does not foretell that the place will be taken?

It was not very difficult to discover that respect and money might be drawn from the multitude by playing the prophet, and the credulity of the people must be a revenue for any who knew how to cheat them. There were in all places soothsayers; but it was not sufficient to foretell in their own name, it was necessary to speak in the name of the divinity; and from the time of the prophets of Egypt, who called themselves seers, till the time of Ulpius, who was prophet to the favorite of the empire, Adrian, who became a god, there was a prodigious number of sacred quacks, who made the gods speak, to make a jest of man. It is well known how they might succeed; sometimes by an ambiguous reply, which they afterwards explained as they pleased; at other times, by corrupting servants, and thereby penetrating the secrets of those devotees, who came to consult them. An idiot was greatly astonished that a cheat should tell him of what he had done in the most hidden manner.

These prophets were reckoned to know the past, the

present, and the future: this is the elogium which Homer makes upon Calchas. I shall add nothing in this place to what the learned Vandale and the judicious Fontenelle his reviser, have said of oracles; they have sagaciously convicted the ages of imposture; and the Jesuit Balthus displayed very little sense, or much malignity, when he supported, in opposition to them, the truth of the Pagan oracles, upon the principles of the Christian religion. It was really doing God an injury, to suppose this God of goodness and truth had let loose the devils from hell, to come upon earth, and there perform what he does not exercise himself, in order to produce oracles.

Either these devils uttered truths, and in that case it was impossible not to believe them, and God himself supporting every kind of false religion by daily miracles, gave the world up to his enemy's will; or else they spoke false; and in this case, God must have unfettered the devils to deceive all mankind. There never was, perhaps, a more absurd opinion.

The most famous oracle was that of Delphos. They at first chose innocent young girls, as more proper than any other to be inspired; that is to say, to utter with faith, all the nonsense the priests dictated to them. The young Pythia mounted a tripod, fixed in the opening of a cavity, from whence a prophetic exhalation issued. The divine spirit made its way under the robe of the Pythia by a channel that is quite human; but a young Pythia having been run away with by a devotee, an old woman supplied the young one's place to carry on the trade; and I believe, that upon this account, the oracle of Delphos began to lose much of its credit.

Divinations and auguries were a kind of oracle, and are, I believe, of higher antiquity; for many ceremonies were necessary, much time was required, to draw custom to a divine oracle, that could not do without a temple and priests; and nothing was easier than to tell fortunes in the cross-ways. This art was subdivided into a thousand shapes; predictions were extracted from the flight of birds, sheep's livers, the lines of the palm of the hand, circles drawn upon the ground, water fire, small flints, wands, and, in a word, from every thing that could be devised, and frequently from enthusiasm alone, which supplied the place of all rules. But who invented this art? The first rogue that met with a fool.

The greatest part of the predictions were like those of the Liege Almanac; "A great man will depart this life. Storms will arise." Does a village magistrate die within a twelvemonth? this was the great man, with respect to that village, whose death was foretold. Is a fishing boat stranded? these are the violent storms predicted. The author of the Liege Almanac is a sorcerer, whether his predictions are or are not accomplished; for if any event favors them, his magic is demonstrated; if the events are opposite, the prediction is applied to a quite different thing, and he saves himself allegorically.

The Liege Almanac has told us that there would come a people from the North, who would destroy every thing; this people did not come, but a north wind froze up some vines, this was what was predicted by Matthew Lansberg. Does any one dare to doubt of his knowledge? the hawkers would as soon arraign him for a bad citizen, or the astrologers treat him as a man of shallow parts and little reason.

The Mahometan Sunnites have greatly availed themselves of this method, in their explanation of Mahomet's Koran. Aldebaran's star was in great veneration amongst the Arabians, it signifies the ox's eye; this meant that Mahomet's eye would enlighten the Arabians, and that, like an ox, he would strike his enemies with his horns.

The acacia tree was in esteem in Arabia; great hedges were made of it, to preserve the crops from the heat of the sun; Mahomet is the acacia, who is to cover the earth with his salutary shade. The sensible Turks laugh at these subtle stupidities; the young women do not think about them; the old female devotees firmly believe them; and he who should say to a dervish, that he teaches nonsense, would run the risk of being impaled. There have been learned men who have traced the history of their own times in the Iliad and Odyssey; but these learned men did not acquire the same fortune as the commentators of the Koran.

The most brilliant function of the oracles was to insure victory in war. Each army, each nation, had its own peculiar oracles, who promised triumphs. The oraculous intelligence of one of the parties was infallibly true. The vanquished, who had been deceived, attributed their defeat to some fault committed towards the gods, after the oracle had been consulted, and they hoped the oracle's prediction would another time be accomplished. Thus is almost the whole earth fed with illusion. There were scarce any people who did not preserve in their archives, or who had not, by oral tradition, some prediction which insured them the conquest of the world, that is to say, of the neighboring nations. No conqueror ever gained a victory, without its being predicted in form, as soon as the battle was over. Even the Jews, who were shut up in a corner of the earth, almost unknown, between Anti-libanus and Arabia Deserta and Petraea, hoped, like the other people, to be the masters of the universe, upon the foundation of a thousand oracles, which we explain in a mystical sense, but which they understood quite literally.

XXXII

OF THE SIBYLS AMONGST THE GREEKS, AND OF THEIR INFLUENCE UPON OTHER NATIONS

WHEN ALMOST the whole earth was crammed with oracles, there were old maids, who, without belonging to any temple, thought proper to prophesy upon their own account. They were called Sibyls, a Greek word of the Laconic dialect, which signified council of God. According to antiquity, there were ten chiefs of them in different countries. The story of the good woman, who came to Rome and brought the ancient Tarquin the nine books of the ancient Sibyls of Cuma, is pretty well known. As Tarquin bargained too much, the old woman threw the six first books into the fire, and insisted upon as much money for the three remaining ones as she had asked for the nine all together. Tarquin paid her. They were, it is said, preserved at Rome, till the time of Sylla, when they were consumed in the conflagration of the Capitol.

But how could the prophecies of the Sibyls be dispensed with? Three senators were dispatched to Erythraea, a city of Greece, where a thousand bad Grecian verses were preciously kept, because they were reputed to be the production of the Sibyl of Erythraea. Every one was anxious to obtain copies of them; the Sibyl of Erythraea had foretold every thing. Her prophecies were considered in the same light as

138

those of Nostradamus with us. Upon every remarkable event, some Greek verses were forged, which were attributed to the Sibyl.

Augustus, who had just reason to fear that in these rhapsodies some verses would be met with that authorized conspiracies, forbade, upon pain of death, any Roman to keep Sibyline verses by him: a prohibition worthy of a suspicious tyrant, who, by address, preserved a power usurped by crimes.

The Sibyline verses were in greater esteem than ever when the reading of them was forbid. They must needs have container truths, as they were concealed to the citizens.

Virgil, in his eclogue upon the birth of Pollio, or Marcellus, or Drusus, failed not to cite the authority of the Sibyl of Cuma, who had fairly foretold that the child who should soon after die, would restore the golden age. The Sibyl of Erythraea had, as it was then said, prophesied at Cuma. The prediction of the new-born infant belonging to Augustus, or to his favorite, must necessarily have taken place. Besides, predictions are never made but for the great; the vulgar are unworthy of them.

These oracles of the Sibyls, being then always in great reputation, the first Christians being too much carried away by false zeal, imagined that they might forge similar oracular predictions, in order to defeat the Gentiles with their own arms. Hermas and St. Justin are reputed the first who supported this imposture. St. Justin cites the oracles of the Sibyl of Cuma, promulgated by a Christian, who had taken the name of Istapus, and pretended that his Sibyl had lived

139

in the time of the deluge.* St. Clement of Alexandria, in his Stormates, assures us that the apostle St. Paul recommends in his epistles, "the reading of the Sibyls, who have manifestly foretold the birth of the son of God."

These epistles of St. Paul must necessarily be lost; for none of these words, nor any like them, are to be found in any of the epistles of St. Paul. An infinite number of books, which we are now no longer possessed of, were then dispersed amongst the Christians, such as the prophecies of Jaldabasth, those of Seth, Enoch, and Kamla; Adam's penances; the history of Zachariah, father to St. John; the evangelist of the Egyptians, the evangelist of St. Peter, of Andrew, of James, the evangelist of Eve, Apocalypse of Adam, the letters of Jesus Christ, and a hundred other writings, of which remain scarce any fragments; and these are buried in books that are very rarely read.

The Christian religion was then divided into a Jewish society, and a Non-Jewish society. These two were subdivided into many others. Whoever was possessed of any degree of talents wrote for his party. There were upwards of fifty evangelists till the council of Nicea; and at present, there remain only those of the Virgin, the Infancy, and Nicodemus. Verses attributed to the Sibyls were particularly forged. Such was the respect the people paid for these Sibylline oracles, that this foreign support was judged necessary to strengthen the dawn of Christianity. Not only Greek Sibylline verses were made, which foretold Jesus Christ; but they were formed in acrostics, so that the letters of these words, *Jesous Chreistos ios Soter,* followed each other

* Strom, lib. 6.

140

at the beginning of every verse. Amongst these poems we meet with this prediction:

> With five loaves and two fishes,
> He shall nourish five thousand men in the desert,
> And by collecting the morsels that remain,
> He shall fill twelve baskets.

They did not confine themselves to this: it was imagined that the sense of the verses of the fourth eclogue of Virgil might be turned in favor of Christianity.

> *Ultima Cumaei venit jam carminis aetas:*
> *Sam nova progenies coelo demittitur alto.*

> The base degenerate iron offspring ends;
> A golden progeny from heav'n descends.

This opinion was so much circulated in the first ages of the church, that the emperor Constantine vehemently supported it. When an emperor spoke he was surely in the right. Virgil was, for a long time, considered as a prophet. The oracles of the Sibyls were at length so thoroughly believed, that in one of our hymns, which is not very ancient, we have these two remarkable verses.

> *Solvet saeculum in favilla*
> *Teste David cum Sibylla.*

> He will reduce the universe to ashes,
> As David and the Sibyl testify.

Amongst the productions attributed to the Sibyls, the Millennium was particularly esteemed and which was

adopted by the fathers of the church, till the time of Theodosius the seecond.

This Millennium of Jesus Christ upon earth, was at first
founded on the prophecy of St. Luke (chap. xxi) a prophecy
that has been misunderstood, "that Jesus would come in the
clouds with great power and majesty, before the present
generation was gone." The generation had passed; but St.
Paul had also said in his first epistle to the Thessalonians,
chap. iv "For this we say unto you, by the word of the Lord,
that we which are alive, and remain unto the coming of
the Lord, shall not prevent them which are asleep. For the
Lord himself shall descend from heaven with a shout, with
the voice of the archangel, and with the trump of God: and
the dead in Christ shall rise first: Then we which are alive
and remain shall be caught up together with them in the
clouds, to meet the Lord in the air: and so shall we ever
be with the Lord."

It is very strange that Paul says, that the Lord himself
spoke unto him; for Paul, so far from having been one of
the disciples of Christ, had for a long time been one of his
persecutors. Though he might be one, the Apocalypse also
said, chap. xx, "that the just should reign upon earth for
a thousand years with Jesus Christ."

It was therefore every moment expected that Jesus Christ
would descend from heaven to establish his reign, and re-
build Jerusalem, wherein the Christians were to rejoice with
the patriarchs.

This new Jerusalem was foretold in the Apocalypse. "I
John, saw the new Jerusalem, which descended from heaven,
decked out like a bride.—It had a large and high wall,

twelve gates, and an angel at each gate—twelve foundations,
—whereon are to be inscribed the names of the apostles of
the lamb—He that spake unto me had a golden fathom to
measure—the city, the gates, and the wall. The city is a
square building, twelve thousand furlongs in circumference;
its length, breadth, and height, are all equal.—He also meas-
ured with it the wall, which is a hundred and forty-four
cubits high—this wall was made of jasper, and the city was
made of gold, etc."

This prediction might have sufficed; but a voucher was
thought necessary, who was a Sibyl, and made to say nearly
the same things. This belief was so strongly imprinted on
the people's minds, that St. Justin in his Dialogue against
Triphon, says, "he is convinced, and that Jesus is to come
into that Jerusalem, and drink and eat with his disciples."

St. Ireneus so completely adopted this opinion, that he
attributes these words to St. John the Evangelist. "In new
Jerusalem every vine shall produce ten thousand branches,
and every branch ten thousand buds, and every bud ten
thousand bunches, and every bunch ten thousand grapes,
and every grape ten thousand amphors of wine. And when
any of the holy vintagers shall gather a grape, the next grape
shall say to him, Take me, I am better than him."*

It was not sufficient that the Sibyl had predicted those
miracles,—there were witnesses of their being fulfilled. Tertullian relates, that the new Jerusalem was seen forty successive nights to descend from heaven.

Tertullian expresses himself thus:† "We confess that

* Ireneus, chap. xxv. b.v.
† Tert. against Marcion. b. 3.

143

the kingdom is promised to us for a thousand years upon earth, after the resurrection in the city of Jerusalem brought down from heaven thither."

Thus has a love of the marvelous, and a desire of hearing and speaking extraordinary things, at all times, perverted common sense. Thus has fraud been brought into play, when force could not be produced. The Christian religion was, in other respects, supported by such solid reasons, that all this jumble of errors could not shake it. The pure gold was extracted from this alloy, and the church, by degrees, arrived at the state where we now see it.

XXXIII

OF MIRACLES

LET US never lose sight of the nature of man: it loves nothing but what is extraordinary, and this is so true, that as soon as the beautiful and sublime become familiar, they are no longer beautiful and sublime. We require uncommon things of every kind; and, in this pursuit, we break down the fences of possibility. Ancient history resembles the history of the cabbage, which was larger than a house, and of the pot, bigger than a church, in which it was to be boiled.

What idea have we affixed to the word *miracle,* which at first signified something admirable? We have said, that what nature cannot produce is contrary to all its laws. So the Englishman, who promised the people of London to get whole into a quart bottle, promised a miracle. And legend-makers would not formerly have been wanting to affirm the accomplishment of this prodigy, if it had produced any thing to the convent.

We believe, without difficulty, the real miracles operated in our holy religion, and amongst the Jews, whose religion paved the way for ours. We speak in this place only of other nations, and we reason only according to the rules of good sense, ever subordinate to revelation.

Whoever is wanting in the light of faith, cannot consider a miracle as any thing else than a contradiction to the eternal laws of nature. It does not appear possible to him that God should disturb his own work: he knows that everything in nature is concatenated by indissoluble chains. He knows that God being immutable, his laws are the same, and that no one wheel of the whole machine can be stopped, without nature's self being disordered.

If Jupiter in lying with Alcmena makes a night of twenty-four hours, when it should consist of only twelve, the earth must necessarily be stopped in its course, and remain motionless twelve whole hours. But as the usual phenomena appeared the succeeding night, the moon and the other plants must consequently have been stopped in their course. This would have been a very great revolution in the celestial orbs, in favor of a woman of Thebes in Boeotia.

A dead man comes to life after being breathless for some days; all the imperceptible particles of his body, which were exhaled in the air, and which had been carried away by the wind, must have returned exactly to their former station, and the worms, birds, or other animals, which were nourished with the substance of this carcass, must each of them restore what he had taken from it. The worms, fattened with the intrails of this man, must have been eaten by swallows, these swallows by magpies, these magpies by falcons, and these falcons by vultures. Each one must restore precisely what belonged to the corpse, without which it could not be the same person. And all this is nothing, without the soul returns to its former mansion.

If the Eternal Being, who has foreseen all things, arranged all things, who governs all things by immutable laws, acts contrary to his own design by subverting those laws,

146

this can be only supposed to take place for the benefit of all nature. But it appears contradictory to suppose a single case, wherein the creator and master of all things, could change the order of the world for the benefit of the world; for he either foresaw the supposed necessity there would be before the change, or else he did not see it. If he did foresee, the necessary regulations were made in the beginning; if he did not foresee, he is no longer God.

It is averred that to please a nation, a city, or a family, the Supreme Being made Pelops, Hippolytus, Heres, and some other famous personages rise from the dead; but it does not seem probable, that the common master of the universe should forget the care of that universe, in favor of this Hippolytus, or this Pelops.

The more incredible miracles are (according to our weak intellects) the more readily they have met with belief. Every people had so many prodigies, that they became very common things; nor did they think it prudent to deny those of their neighbors. The Greeks said to the Egyptians and Asiatic nations, the gods spoke to you sometimes, they speak to us every day; if they have fought twenty times for you, they have put themselves forty times at the head of our armies. If you have metamorphoses, we have a hundred times more than you. If your animals speak, ours have made very elegant orations. There are no people, even down to the Romans, among whom beasts, have not had the power of speech, to foretell future events. Titus Livius relates, that an ox cried out in the public market-place when full of people, "Rome take care of thyself." Pliny in his eighth book says, that a dog spoke, when Tarquin was driven from

147

the throne. If Suetonius is to be credited, a crow cried out in the Capitol, when Domitian was going to be assassinated, *Estai panta Kalos,* very well done, *all is well.* In the same manner one of Achilles's horses, named Xante, foretold to his master that he should fall before Troy. Before Achilles's horse, Phrixus's ram had spoke, as well as the cows upon Mount Olympus. So that instead of refuting fables, they were improved upon. This was like the counsel whose client had a bond forged upon him; he did not amuse himself with pleadings, he immediately produced a forged receipt.

It is true we do not meet with many resurrections amongst the Romans; they confined themselves to miraculous cures. The Greeks, more attached to the metempsychosis, had many resurrections. They had this secret from the people of the East, from whom all science and superstition are derived.

Of all the miraculous cures, the best attested, and most authentic, are those of the blind man, whom the emperor Vespasian restored to sight, and the paralytic who by this monarch's aid recovered the use of his limbs. It is in Alex-andria that this double miracle operates, before innumerable spectators, before Romans, Greeks, and Egyptians. It is upon his tribunal, that Vespasian operates these prodigies. He does not endeavor to gain esteem by imposture, which is unnecessary to a monarch who is firmly seated on his throne: but the two patients prostrate themselves at his feet, and conjure him to cure them; he blushes at their entreaties, ridicules them, saying that such cures are not in the power of mortals. They insist upon it: Serapis has appeared to them; Serapis has told them they shall be cured by Vespasian. He at length lets himself be prevailed upon; he touches them

148

without being flattered with success. The divinity, favoring his modesty and virtue, communicates to Vespasian his power; that instant the blind man sees, and the lame one walks. Alexandria, Egypt, all the empire, applaud Vespasian, favored by heaven. The miracle is preserved in the archives of the empire, and in all the contemporary histories. This miracle has nevertheless in course of time been disbelieved by every one, because no one is interested in supporting its credit.

If we believe I know not what sort of a writer of our barbarous ages, named *Helgaut,* king Robert, son to Hughes Capet, also cured a blind man. This miraculous gift was probably given to Robert, to requite the charity wherewith he burnt his wife's confessor, and the canons of Orleans, who were accused of not believing the infallibility and absolute power of the pope, and consequently of being Manicheans; or if this was not the recompense of this good action, it was to indemnify him, for the excommunication which he suffered, for lying with the queen his wife.

Philosophers have made miracles in the same manner as emperors and kings. We are acquainted with those of Apollonius Tyaneus; he was a Pythagorian philosopher, temperate, chaste, and just, who is not reproached by history with any equivocal action, nor any of those weaknesses with which Socrates is stigmatized. He travelled amongst the Magi and the Bramins; and was the more honored everywhere, on account of his modesty, incessantly giving wise counsel, and seldom disputing. The constant prayer, which he preferred to the gods, was admirable: "Immortal gods, grant unto us what you think is needful, and which we are not unworthy

149

of." He was no enthusiast; but his disciples were enthusiasts; they attributed miracles to him, which were collected by Philostrates, The Tyraneans placed him amongst the demigods, and the Roman emperors approved of his apotheosis. But in time, the apotheosis of Apollonius had the same fate as that which was decreed the Roman emperors; and the chapel of Apollonius was equally deserted as the Socrateion, which was erected by the Athenians to Socrates.

The kings of England from the time of St. Edward, to the time of William III daily performed a great miracle, which was to cure the evil, which physicians could not remove. But William III would perform no miracles, and his successors have followed his example in abstaining from them. If England should ever undergo any great revolution whereby that nation will be sunk again in ignorance, the English will then have miracles operated every day.

XXXIV

OF THE TEMPLES

TEMPLES WERE not erected so soon as a God was acknowledged. The Arabians, the Chaldeans, the Persians, who revered the stars, could scarce have consecrated edifices immediately; they could only look up to heaven: this was their temple. That of Bel at Babylon is esteemed the most ancient of all; but those of Brama in India must be of more remote antiquity; this is, at least, supposed by the Bramins.

We find in the annals of China, that the first emperors sacrificed in a temple. That of Hercules at Tyre does not appear to be amongst the most ancient. Hercules was never considered by any people, but as a secondary divinity: the temple of Tyre is of much anterior date to that of Judea. Hiram had a very magnificent one, when Solomon, assisted by Hiram, built his own. Herodotus, who traveled amongst the Tyrians, says, that in his time, according to the archives of Tyre, the antiquity of this temple was but two thousand three hundred years. Egypt was full of temples for a long time. Herodotus also says, that the temple of Vulcan at Memphis had been erected by Menes about the time that corresponds to three thousand years before our era: and it is incredible that the Egyptians had erected a temple to Vulcan, before they had bestowed one upon Isis, their principal divinity.

151

I cannot reconcile with the common manners of men what Herodotus says in his second book; he avers that it was customary with all the other people, except the Egyptians and the Greeks, to lie with their wives in the middle of their temples. I suspect, that the Greek text has been corrupted; the most savage of men abstain from this action before witnesses. No man was ever known to caress his wife, or his mistress, in the presence of any for whom he had the smallest regard.

It is scarce possible that amongst so many nations, who were the most scrupulously religious, all the temples should be places of prostitution. I believe Herodotus meant to say, that the priests who inhabited the enclosure which surrounded the temple might lie with their wives in that enclosure, which was called the temple, as did the Jewish, and other priests; but that the Egyptian priests, who did not dwell within that enclosure, abstained from touching their wives when they were upon guard in the porches with which the temple was surrounded.

The people who were less numerous were a long time before they had temples. They carried their gods in boxes and tabernacles. We have already seen, that when the Jews inhabited the eastern deserts of the lake Asphaltides, they carried the tabernacle of the god Rempham, of the god Moloc, of the god Kiam, according to Jeremiah, Amos, and St. Stephen.

This custom was practiced by all the little nations of the Desert. This usage must be the most ancient of any, because it is much easier to have a box than to erect a great edifice.

These portable gods, probably, gave rise to the custom of processions, which took place with every nation: for it appears that it would not have been judged right to take a god out of his place in his temple, to carry him about the city; and his violence might have been looked upon as a sacrilege, if the ancient custom of carrying one's gods in a cart, or upon a litter, had not been for a long time established.

The greatest part of the temples were, at first, citadels, wherein sacred things were securely deposited. Thus the Palladium was in the fortress of Troy; and the bucklers which descended from heaven were kept in the Capitol.

We find that the temple of the Jews was a strong house capable of sustaining an assault. It is said in the third book of Kings, that the edifice was sixty cubits in length, and twenty in breadth, which is about ninety feet long and thirty wide. There are scarce any public edifices smaller. But this house being built of stone, upon a mountain, might, at least, defend itself against a surprise; the windows, which were much smaller without than within, looked like slaughtering holes.

It is said that the priests lodged in wooden sheds, supported by the wall.

It is difficult to comprehend the dimensions of this architecture. We are told in the same book of Kings, that upon the walls of this temple there were three wooden floors: that the first was five cubits wide, the second six, and the third seven. These proportions are not the same as ours: these floors would have astonished Michelangelo and Bradamante. Be this as it may, it should be considered, that this temple was built upon the declivity of the mountain of

Moria, and consequently that it could not be of any great depth. A person must have went up several steps before he could gain the little esplanade, where stood the long sanctuary of twenty cubits. Now a temple wherein a person must go up and down is a barbarous edifice. It was to be admired for its sanctity; but not for its architecture. It was not necessary to accomplish God's designs, that the city of Jerusalem was to be the most magnificent of all cities, and his people the most powerful of all people; nor was it necessary that its temple should surpass that of all other nations: the finest temple is that wherein the purest devotions are paid to him.

The greatest part of commentators have taken the trouble to delineate this edifice, each in his own way. There is reason to believe, that not one of these draftsmen ever built a house. We conceive however, that these walls which supported these three floors being stone, people might make a defense in this little retreat, for two or three days.

This little fortress of a people deprived of arts did not hold out against Nabuzardam, one of the captains of the king of Babylon, whom we call Nabuchodnosor or Nabuchaednosor.

The second temple erected by Nehemiah was neither so great nor sumptuous. We learn in the book of Esdras, that the walls of this new temple had only three rows of rough stone, and that the rest was of wood only. It was rather a barn than a temple. But that which Herod afterwards built was a real fortress. He was obliged, as Josephus tells us, to demolish the temple of Nehemiah, which he calls the temple of Aggea. Herod fitted up part of the precipice, at the bottom of the mountain of Moria, to make a platform, which was supported by a very thick wall, whereupon the temple was erected. Near this edifice stood the tower of Antonia, which he again fortified; so that this temple was a real citadel.

In effect, the Jews had resolution enough to defend them-selves against Titus's army, till a Roman soldier having thrown in a flaming piece of timber, the whole edifice imme-diately took fire. This proves that the internal buildings of the temple consisted of nothing but wood in the time of Herod, as well as in the reigns of Nehemiah and Solomon.

These fir buildings are somewhat contradictory to that magnificence which Josephus, so fond of exaggerating, speaks of. He says, that Titus having entered into the sanctuary admired it, and owned that its riches surpassed its fame. It is not very probable that a Roman emperor, in the midst of carnage, marching over heaps of slain, should amuse himself in considering with admiration an edifice twenty cubits long, as was the sanctuary; and that a man who had seen the Capitol should be surprised at the magnificence of a Jewish temple. This temple was doubtless very holy; but a sanctuary twenty cubits long was not built by a Vitruvius. The fine temples were those of Ephesus, Alexandria, Athens, Olympus, and Rome.

Josephus, in his declamation against Appion, says, "that the Jews wanted only one temple, because there is but one God." This reasoning does not appear conclusive; for if the country of the Jews, like that of many other people, had been seven or eight hundred miles in circumference, they must have passed their whole lives in travelling, to sacrifice in this temple once a year. It follows from there being only one God, that all the temples of the world should be dedicated to him only; but it does not follow, that there should be only one temple upon earth. Superstition is always supported by false logic.

Besides, how could Josephus say that the Jews wanted only one temple, when they had from the reign of Ptolemy Philometor a temple well enough known, of the *Onion*, at Bubastis in Egypt?

XXXV

OF MAGIC

WHAT IS magic? The secret of doing what nature cannot perform; what is impossible: yet magic has at all times gained credit. The word is derived from the *Mag, Magdim,* or magi of Chaldea. They knew more than other people; they sought for the cause of rain and fine weather; and they were soon reckoned to be the makers of rain and fine weather. They were astronomers; the most ignorant and daring were astrologers. An event happened under the junc- tion of two planets, these two planets had therefore pro- duced this event; and the astrologers were the masters of the planets. Distempered imaginations had in a dream seen their friends dying or dead: the magicians made the departed friends appear.

Having discovered the course of the moon, they could easily make the moon take a trip down upon earth. They also disposed of the life of man either by figures of wax, or by pronouncing the name of God or the devil. Clement of Alexandria in his Stromates, book v says, that according to an ancient author, Moses pronounced the name Ihaho, or Jehovah, so effectually to the ear of Phara Nekefr, king of Egypt, that he died upon the spot.

In fine, from the time of Jannes and Membres, who were the patent sorcerers of Pharaoh, till that of La Marechale

D'Ancre, who was burnt at Paris, for killing a white cock when it was full moon, there was not any period destitute of sorcery.

The Pythoness of Endor who raised the ghost of Samuel is very well known; it is true there is something strange that the word *Python,* which is Greek, should be known to the Jews, in the time of Saul. Many learned men have concluded from hence that this history was not written, till the Jews traded with the Greeks, after the time of Alexander; but this is not the point in question here.

To return to magic: the Jews carried on the trade as soon as they were dispersed over the world. The sorcerer's sabbath is an evident proof of this: and the he-goat, with which the sorceresses were supposed to have copulated, is derived from the ancient correspondence the Jews had with goats in the Desert, with which they are reproached in Leviticus, chap. xvii.

There are scarce any criminal prosecutions carried on amongst us for sorcery, without some Jews being impeached.

The Romans, as enlightened as they were in the time of Augustus, were still infatuated with sorcery, as we are. See Virgil's Eclogue, entitled *Pharmacentria.*

Carmina vel coelo possunt deducere lunam.

The voice of the enchanter brings down the moon.

His ego saepe lupum fieri & se condere silvis.
Maerim saepe animas imis exire sepulchris.

   Smear'd with these pow'rful juices, on the plain
He howls a wolf among the hungry train:
And oft the mighty necromancer boasts,
With these, to call from tombs the stalking ghosts.

People are astonished that Virgil to this day passes for a sorcerer at Naples. There is no occasion to seek for the reason any where but in this Eclogue.

Horace reproaches Sagana and Canidia with their abominable sorcery. The first heads of the republic were infected with these shocking notions. Sextus, son to Pompey the Great, immolated a child in one of these enchantments.

Philters were charms of a less violent nature, that they might gain more admirers: the Jews were the proprietors of them, and sold them to the Roman ladies. Such of that nation as could not become rich brokers fabricated prophecies or philters.

All these extravagances, ridiculous impositions, or shocking impostures, are perpetuated amongst ourselves; and no age has discredited them. Missionaries have been astonished to find these extravagances at the extremities of the world, and they have complained to the people whom the demon had inspired with them. Why, my friends, did you not remain in your own country? You would not, indeed, have met with more devils there; but you would have found every whit as much nonsense.

You would have seen thousands of wretches insensible enough to believe themselves sorcerers, and judges stupid and barbarous enough to condemn them to the flames; you would have seen a jurisprudence in Europe founded on magic, in the same manner as there are laws against theft and murder; a jurisprudence established upon the decision of councils. What was still worse, was, that the people finding the magistracy of the church believed in magic, they were only the more invincibly persuaded of its existence; and consequently

159

the more sorcerers were persecuted, the more numerous they became. Whence arose so fatal and general an error? From ignorance; and this evinces that those who undeceive men are their greatest benefactors.

It has been said, that the universal consent of all men was the test of truth. What a proof! Every people has believed in magic, in astrology, in oracles, in lunar influences. It should at least have been said, that the consent of all wise men was not a proof, but a kind of probability! did not all the sages before Copernicus believe, that the earth was motionless, and fixed in the center of the world?

No one people have a right to ridicule another; if Rabelais calls Picatrix, "my reverend father in the devil," because magic was taught at Toledo, Salamanca, and Seville, the Spaniards may retort upon the French the prodigious number of their sorcerers.

France is, perhaps, of all countries that which has the most blended cruelty and ridicule. There is not a single tribunal in France, that has not burnt many magicians. In ancient Rome there were madmen who fancied themselves sorcerers; but we do not find any barbarians that burnt them.

XXXVI

OF HUMAN VICTIMS

MEN WOULD have been too happy if they had only been deluded; but time, whereby customs are alternately corrupted and rectified, having shed the blood of animals upon the altar, the butchering priests, habitually sanguinary, changed from animals to man; and superstition, the natural daughter of religion, so far forsook her mother's purity, as to compel men to sacrifice their own children, under the pretense that we should give to God what was the dearest to us.

The first sacrifice of this nature, if the fragments of Sanchoniaton are to be credited, was that of Jehud amongst the Phenicians, who was immolated by his father Hillu, about two thousand years before our era. The great states were at this time already established; Syria, Chaldea, and Egypt, were very flourishing, and Herodotus says, that a young woman was so early drowned in the Nile, to obtain a more abundant flux of this river, which was neither too rapid nor too feeble.

These abominable sacrifices made their way almost over the whole earth. Pausanias asserts, that Lycaon immolated the first of his human victims in Greece. This custom must have been received in the time of the Trojan war, as Homer makes Achilles immolate twelve Trojans to Patrocles's shade. Would Homer have dared assert so terrible a thing? Would

161

he not have feared disgusting all his readers, if sacrifices had not been in use?

I do not speak of the sacrifice of Iphigenia, or that of Idamante, son to Idomeneus: whether true or false they prove the reigning opinion. The sacrifices which the Taurian Scythians made of strangers cannot be doubted.

If we descend to more modern times, the Tyrians and Carthaginians, when in imminent danger, sacrificed a man to Saturn. The same was done in Italy; and the Romans themselves, who condemned these horrid proceedings, immolated two Gauls and two Greeks, to expiate a vestal's crime. This is what Plutarch teaches us, in his Questions upon the Romans.

This horrid custom prevailed amongst the Gauls and Germans. The Druids burnt human victims in large ozier figures. Amongst the Germans, sorcerers cut the throats of those who were devoted to death, and judged of futurity by the greater or less rapidity of the blood which issued from the wound.

I believe these sacrifices did not often happen. If they had been made annual festivals, if every family had been in perpetual apprehension of their handsomest girl or oldest boy being chosen, to have their hearts sacredly torn out upon a consecrated stone, this would soon have been put an end to, by immolating the priests themselves. It is very probable, that these holy parricides were not committed but upon very urgent occasions, in times of imminent danger, when men are conquered by fear, and when the false idea of public interest silenced all private considerations.

Amongst the Bramins, every widow did not burn herself

162

upon her husband's corpse. The most devout and rash have from time immemorial made, and still make, this astonishing sacrifice. The Scythians sometimes immolated to the manes of their Kans the most favorite officers of these princes. Herodotus says they were impaled round the royal corpse; but it does not appear by history this custom prevailed for any length of time.

If we read the history of the Jews written by an author of another nation, we shall with difficulty believe, that there ever really was a fugitive people of Egypt, who came by the express order of God to immolate seven or eight small nations whom they did not know; to slay without mercy all the women, all the old men, and even the children at the breast, reserving none but the little girls; that this holy people were punished by their God, when they were so criminal as to save a single man, who was anathematized. We could not believe that so abominable a race could exist upon earth. But as this very people relate all these facts themselves in their holy books, they must be believed.

I shall not here discuss the question, whether these books were inspired. Our holy church, which looks with horror upon the Jews, teaches us that these Jewish books were dictated by God, the creator and father of all men; I cannot form the least doubt about it, nor allow myself in any shape to reason upon it.

It is true that our feeble understanding cannot conceive in God any other wisdom, any other justice, any other goodness, than those of which we have the idea: but, in fine, he has done all he pleased; it is not for us to judge him; I constantly confine myself to mere history.

163

The Jews have a law, whereby they are expressly ordered to spare nothing nor any man devoted to the Lord: "He cannot be bought off, he must die," according to the law of Leviticus, chap. xxvii. It is by virtue of this law that we find Jephtha sacrifices his own daughter, and the priest Samuel cuts into morsels king Agag. The Pentateuch tells us, that in the little country of Midian, which contains about nine square leagues, the Israelites, having found six hundred seventy-five thousand sheep, seventy-two thousand oxen, sixty-one thousand asses, and thirty-two thousand virgins, Moses commanded that all the men, all the women, and all the children, should be massacred; and that all the maids should be preserved, and thirty-two only of them were immolated. The remarkable part of this acknowledgment is, that this same Moses was a kinsman of Jethro, the high-priest of the Midianites, who had done him the most signal services, and heaped kindnesses upon him.

The same book tells us, that Joshua, the son of Nun, having passed the river Jordan, with his herd dry-footed, having caused the walls of Jericho, which was anathematized, to fall at the sound of trumpets, that he made all the inhabitants perish in the flames; that he preserved only Rahab, the harlot, and her family, who had concealed the spies of the holy people; that the same Joshua devoted to death twelve thousand inhabitants of the city of Hai; that he sacrificed to the Lord thirty-one kings of the country, who were all anathematized and hanged. We have nothing in our latter times to compare with these religious assassinations, without it be the massacre of St. Bartholomew, and those of Ireland.

It is melancholy that many people doubt the Jews having

found six hundred seventy-five thousand sheep, and thirty-two thousand virgins, in the village of a desert in the midst of rocks, and that no one doubts of the affair of St. Bartholomew. But we cannot too often repeat, how much the lights of our reason are impotent, when we endeavor to elucidate the strange events of antiquity, and clear unto our understandings the reasons why God, master of life and death, chose the Jewish people to exterminate the people of Canaan.

XXXVII

OF THE MYSTERIES OF ELEUSINIA CERES

IN THE chaos of popular superstition, which would have made almost the whole globe one vast den of ferocious animals, there was a salutary institution, which prevented one part of the human species from degenerating into an entire state of brutality: this consisted of mysteries and expiations. It was scarce possible not to find some people of gentle disposition, and sages, amongst so many cruel madmen; or that there should be no philosophers, who should endeavor to bring men back to reason and morality.

Those sages made use of superstition itself to correct its enormous abuses, in the same manner as the heart of a viper is applied to cure its bite; many fables were intermingled with useful truths, and these truths were supported by fable.

The mysteries of Zoroaster are no longer known: we have but very little insight into those of Isis; but we cannot doubt, that they foretold the grand system of a future state; for Celsus says to Origenes, book viii, "You boast of believing in eternal punishments, and did not all the mystical ministers preach them to their initiated?"

God's unity was the principal dogma of all the mysteries. Apuleius has preserved for us the prayer of the priestesses of Isis: "The coelestial powers serve thee; the infernal regions are submitted to thee; the universe revolves in thine hand;

thy feet trample upon Tartarus; the planets answer to thy voice; the seasons return at thy order; the elements obey thee."

The mystical ceremonies of Ceres were an imitation of those of Isis. Those who had committed crimes confessed them and expiated them; they fasted, purified themselves, and gave alms. All the ceremonies were held sacred by solemn oaths, to make them more venerated. The mysteries were celebrated at night, in order to inspire a kind of holy horror. Certain species of tragedies were represented the fable of which set forth the happiness of the just, and the punish- ments of the wicked. The greatest men of antiquity, such as Plato and Cicero, have written eulogia upon these mys- teries, which were not yet degenerated from their primitive purity.

Some very learned men have proved that the sixth book of the Eneid, is only a picture of what was practiced in these secret and famous representations. He does not, indeed, speak of the Demiourgoi, who represented the creator; but in the vestibule, or prelude, he brings on the children whose par- ents had left them to perish; and this was a hint to fathers and mothers. *Continuo auditae voces vagitus & ingens, etc.* Minos afterwards appeared to judge the dead. The wicked were dragged to Tartarus, and the just conducted to the Elysian fields. This garden comprised everything the imagina- tion could suggest for the benefit of mere men. Only heroes and demi-gods obtained the privilege of ascending to heaven. Every religion has suggested a garden for the abode of the just; and even when the Essenians, amongst the Jewish people, received the dogma of a future state, they believed that the good, after death, would go into a garden upon the banks of the sea. As for the Pharisees, they adopted the metempsychosis, and not the resurrection. If it be allowed to quote the sacred history of Jesus Christ, amongst such a variety of profane things, we shall observe, that he says to the penitent thief, "this day shalt thou be with me in the garden."* He conformed himself to the language of all men.

The mysteries of Eleusinia became the most celebrated. One very remarkable thing is, that they there read the beginning of the theogony of Sanchoniaton the Phoenician; this is a proof that Sanchoniaton had preached one supreme God, creator and governor of the world. It was then that this doctrine was unveiled to the initiated, instructed in the belief of polytheism. Let us image to ourselves a superstitious people, who were accustomed from their earliest infancy to pay the same worship to the virgin, St. Joseph, and the other saints, as to God the father. It would perhaps be dangerous to disabuse them all on a sudden; it would at first be prudent to reveal only to the most moderate and rational the infinite distance there is between God and his creatures. This was precisely the system of the mystagogues. Those who participated of the mysteries assembled in the temple of Ceres, and the Hierophanta taught them, that instead of adoring Ceres leading Triptolemus upon a car drawn by dragons, they should adore that God who nourished men, and permitted Ceres and Triptolemus to render agriculture so honorable.

This is so true, that the Hierophanta began by reciting the ancient verses of Orpheus: "Walk in the path of justice;

* St. Luke, chap. xxiii.

168

adore the sole master of the universe; he is one, he is singly by himself; to him all beings owe their existence; he acts in them and by them; he sees all, and never was seen by mortal eyes."

I acknowledge I do not conceive how Pausanias can say that these verses are not as estimable as those of Homer; it must be agreed, at least, that with respect to sense they are of more intrinsic value than the Iliad and Odyssey together.

The learned bishop Warburton, though very unjust in many of his bold decisions, gives great strength to all that I have been saying of the necessity of concealing the dogma of God's unity to a people headstrong with polytheism. He observes after Plutarch, that the young Alcibiades, having assisted at these mysteries, readily insulted the statues of Mercury in a party of debauchery with several of his friends; and that the people in their rage insisted upon Alcibiades's being condemned.

The greatest direction was therefore then necessary, not to shock the prejudices of the multitude: Alexander himself, having obtained leave in Egypt of the Hierophanta of the mysteries, to acquaint his mother with the secrets of the initiated, at the same time conjured her to burn his letter after reading it, that she might not irritate the Greeks.

Those who, deceived by a false zeal, have since imagined that the mysteries were nothing but infamous debauches ought to be undeceived by the word which answers to *initiated;* it signifies, that they entered upon a new life.

Another indubitable proof that these mysteries were celebrated only to inspire virtue in men is the set form with which the assembly was dismissed. Amongst the Greeks, the two ancient Phenician words *Koff omphet,* Watch and be pure, were pronounced. We may produce, as an additional proof, that the emperor Nero, who was guilty of his mother's death, could not be admitted to these mysteries, when he travelled in Greece; the crime was too enormous; and as great an emperor as he was, the initiated would not receive him amongst them. Zozimus also says, that Constantine could find no Pagan priests who would purify him and absolve him of parricide.

There must then, in fact, have been amongst those people whom we call Pagans, Gentiles, and idolaters, a very pure religion, whilst the people and priests followed shameful customs, trifling ceremonies, ridiculous doctrines, and while they even sometimes shed human blood in honor of some imaginary gods, who were despised and detested by the sages.

This pure religion consisted in acknowledging the existence of a supreme God, his providence and justice. What disfigured these mysteries, if Tertullian is to be credited, was the ceremony of regeneration. It was necessary that the initiated should seem to be re-born; this was the symbol of the new kind of life he was to embrace. He was presented with a crown, and he trampled upon it. The Hierophanta held the sacred knife over his head; the initiated, who feigned to be struck with it, fell as if he were dead; after which he appeared to regenerate. The free-masons still retain a fragment of this ancient ceremony.

Pausanias in his Arcadics tells us, that in several temples of Eleusinia the penitents and initiated were flagellated; an

170

odious custom, which was a long time after introduced in several Christian churches. I doubt not that in all these mysteries, the ground-work of which was so sensible and useful, many censurable superstitions were introduced. Superstition led to debauchery, which brought on contempt. Of all these ancient mysteries, there were at length no other remains, but those gangs of beggars, whom we have seen, under the name of Egyptians and Bohemians, wander all over Europe with castinets, dancing the priests of Isis' dance, selling balm, curing the itch, though covered with it, telling fortunes, and stealing poultry. Such has been the end of what was the most sacred thing of half the known world.

XXXVIII

OF THE JEWS, AT THE TIME THEY BEGAN TO BE KNOWN

WE SHALL touch as little as possible upon what is divine in the history of the Jews; or, if we are compelled to speak of it, we shall go no farther than as their miracles have an essential connection with the sequel of events. We have all the respect that is due to the continual prodigies which signalized all the steps of that nation. We believe them with all the reasonable faith that is required by the church, that is, the substitute to the synagogue; we do not examine them, we constantly confine ourselves to history. We shall talk of the Jews, as we spoke of the Scythians and the Greeks, in weighing the probabilities and discussing the facts. No other persons than themselves having wrote their history, before the Romans destroyed their state, it is only necessary to consult their annals.

This is one of the most modern nations, considering them as the other people only from the time they formed a settle-ment and possessed a capital. The Jews seem to be considered by their neighbors only in the time of Solomon, which was nearly about that of Hesiod and Homer, and the first archons of Athens.

The name of Solomon, or Soleiman, is well known to the Eastern people; but that of David is not, and Saul still less. The Jews before Saul appeared only like a band of Arabs of the Desert, of so little power that the Phenicians treated them nearly in the same manner as the Lacedemonians treated the Ilotes. These were slaves, who were not allowed arms. They had not the privilege of forging iron, not even to sharpen their plow-shares and the edge of their hatchets. They were obliged to apply to their masters for any kind of work of this nature; this is set forth by the Jews in the book of Samuel; and they add, that they had neither sword nor javelin, in the battle which Saul and Jonathan gave as Bethaven against the Phenicians, or Philistines, an action in which it is related of Saul that he made an oath of sacrificing to the Lord he that should eat during the conflict.

It is true that before this battle won without arms, it is said in the preceding chapter,* that Saul with an army of three hundred thirty thousand men entirely defeated the Ammonites; which does not seem to agree with the confes-sion, that they had neither sword nor javelin, nor any other arms. Moreover, the greatest princes have seldom had at one time three hundred thirty thousand effective warriors. How could the Jews, who appear wandering and oppressed in this little country, which has not a single fortified city, no arms, not so much as a sword, be able to bring thirty-three thousand soldiers into the field? These were sufficient to con-quer Asia and Europe. Let us leave the pains of reconciling these apparent contradictions, which superior intellects re-move, to learned and celebrated authors: let us respect what we are obliged to respect; and let us recur to the history of the Jews according to their own writings.

* 1 Kings, chap. ii.

XXXIX

OF THE JEWS IN EGYPT

ACCORDING TO the annals of the Jews, this nation inhabited the confines of Egypt in those remote times that history
furnishes no account of: they resided in the little country
of Gossen, or Gessen, towards mount Casius and lake Sirbon.
The Arabians, who in winter, repair with their herds to
graze in Lower Egypt, still remain there. This nation was
composed of no more than a single family, who, in the space
of four hundred years, produced a race of two millions of
people; for to furnish six hundred thousand warriors, who
according to Genesis came out of Egypt, they must have
consisted of at least two millions of souls. This multiplication, contrary to the order of nature, is one of those miracles
which God deigned to operate in favour of the Jews.

It is in vain for a multitude of learned men to be astonished that the King of Egypt should have commanded the
two midwives to destroy all the male children of the Hebrews;
that the king's daughter who resided at Memphis should go
and bathe herself at a great distance from Memphis, in a
branch of the Nile, where nobody ever bathed, on account
of crocodiles: it is in vain for them to make objections to
the age of eighty, which Moses had already attained, before
he undertook to conduct a whole people out of bondage.

They dispute upon the ten plagues of Egypt; they say

that the magicians of the kingdom could not perform the same miracles as the messenger of God; and that if God gave them his power, he seems to have acted against himself. They suppose, that as Moses had changed all the waters into blood, there remained no more water for the magicians to perform the same metamorphosis upon.

They ask how could Pharaoh pursue the Jews with a great number of horsemen, after all the horses had died, by the fifth and sixth plagues? They ask why six hundred warriors should run away when God was at their head, and they might have engaged the Egyptians to advantage, all the first born of whom being struck dead? They ask again, why God did not give fertile Egypt to his cherished people, instead of making them wander forty years in shocking deserts?

There is but a single answer to all these innumerable objections; and this answer is, God would have it so; the church believes it, and we should believe it. It is in this respect, that this history differs from others. Every people have their prodigies; but every thing is prodigious with the Jewish nation; and it should have been so, as they were conducted by God himself. It is plain that the history of God should not resemble that of men. Wherefore we shall not relate any of those supernatural facts, which should be mentioned only in the holy Scripture. Still less should we dare attempt their explanation. Let us only examine those few that may be subject to criticism.

XL

OF MOSES, CONSIDERED ONLY AS THE CHIEF OF A NATION

THE MASTER of nature only gives strength to the arm which he deigns to choose. Moses is supernatural in every thing. More than one learned man has looked upon him as a very able politician. Others have considered him only as a weak reed, which the divine hand deigned to use, to frame the destiny of empires. What can we think of an old man of eighty years of age, who by himself alone undertakes to conduct a whole people over whom he had no authority? His arm cannot fight, nor his tongue articulate. He is described a cripple and a stammerer. He conducts his followers for forty years successively into horrid deserts. He wants to give them a settlement; but he gives them none. If we were to pursue his steps, in the desert of Sur, Sin, Oreb, Sinai, Phara, Cadesh Barnea, and observe his retrograde motions towards the very spot he set out from, we could not easily conceive that he was a great captain. He is at the head of six hundred thousand warriors, and he could neither provide clothing nor subsistence for his troops. God does all things, God remedies all things, he nourishes, he clothes the people by miracles. Moses, then, is nothing of himself, and his impotence shows, that he can be guided by nothing but the hand of the Almighty; we therefore consider him

176

only as a man, and not the minister of God. His person, in this capacity, is an object of more sublime inquiry.

He wants to go into the country of the Canaanites, on the west of Jordan, in the country of Jericho, which is in fact the only fruitful spot of the whole province; and instead of taking this road, he turns towards the east, between Esiongaber, and the Black Sea, a savage barren country, thick strewed with mountains that do not produce a single shrub, without a rivulet, without a fountain, save a few little wells of salt water. When the news of this eruption of a foreign people reached the Canaanites or Phenicians, they came and gave them battle in these deserts, near Cadesh Barnea. How can he let himself be beat at the head of six hundred thousand soldiers, in a country which does not now contain three thousand inhabitants? At the end of thirty-nine years, he gains two victories, but he does not compass any one object of his legislation: he and his people die before he sets foot in the country which he wanted to conquer.

A legislator, according to our common notions, should make himself beloved and feared; but he should not push severity to barbarity: he should not, instead of inflicting by the ministers of the law some punishments upon the criminal, make a foreign nation murder the greatest part of his own people.

Could Moses at near the age of an hundred and twenty years, being conducted only by himself, have been so inhuman, so hardened in bloodshed, as to command the Levites to massacre indiscriminately their brothers to the number of twenty-three thousand, and, to screen his own brother, who ought rather to have died, than made a golden calf to

177

be adored? And, strange to relate, his brother is after this shameful action created high pontiff, and thirty-three thousand men are massacred.

Moses had wedded a Midianite, daughter to Jethro, high-priest of Midian, in Arabia Petraea: Jethro had heaped kindness upon him: he had bestowed his son upon him, to serve him as a guide in the deserts; what cruelty, contrary to all policy (to judge according to our feeble notions) must Moses have been guilty of, to sacrifice twenty-four thousand men of his own nation, under pretense that a Jew had been found lying with a Midianite? And how can it be said, after such astonishing butchery, "that Moses was the most gentle of all men?" We must acknowledge, humanly speaking, that these horrid deeds revolt against reason and nature. But, if we consider Moses as the minister of God's designs and vengeance, the aspect is entirely changed: he is not a man that acts as a man; he is the instrument of the divinity, whom we should not call to account. We should offer up silent adoration.

If Moses had of himself instituted his religion, like Zoroaster, Thaut, the first Bramins, Numa, Mahomet, and many others, we might ask him, why he did not avail himself of the most useful and efficacious means of restraining lust and sin? why he did not expressly preach the immortality of the soul, rewards and punishments after death; dogmas long before received in Egypt, in Phoenicia, in Mesopotamia, in Persia, and in India? "You have been instructed, we should tell him, in the wisdom of the Egyptians, you are a legislator, and you absolutely neglect the principal dogma of the Egyptians, the most necessary dogma to man, a belief so salutary and holy, that your own Jews, barbarous as they were, embraced it a long time after you; it was, at least, partly adopted by the Esssenes, and the Pharisees, at the end of a thousand years."

This perplexing objection against a common legislator falls to the ground, and loses, as we find, all its force, when a law given by God himself, who condescended being the king of the Jewish people, temporally rewarded and punished them, and who would not reveal the knowledge of the immortality of the soul, and hell's eternal torments, but at the time appointed by his decrees. Almost every event merely human among the Jews is the summit of horror. Everything divine is above our feeble comprehensions. We are constantly silenced by them both.

There have been men of extensive knowledge, who have carried their scepticism so far, as to doubt there having ever existed such a one as Moses; his life, which is a series of prodigies from his cradle to his grave, appeared to them an imitation of the ancient Arabian fables, and particularly that of the ancient Bacchus.* They do not know at what period to fix Moses; even the name of Pharaoh, King of Egypt, is unknown. No monument, no vestige, remains of the country in which he is said to travel. It seems impossible to them, that Moses should have governed two or three millions of men for forty years in uninhabitable deserts, where we can scarce meet at present with two or three gangs of vagabonds, who do not altogether make more than between three and four thousand men. We are far from adopting this bold

* See the article under the head of Bacchus.

179

opinion, which would sap the very foundation of the ancient history of the Jewish people.

Neither shall we adhere to the opinion of Aben Esra, of Maimonides, Nugens, or the author of the Jewish Ceremonies, though the learned Le Clerc, Middleton, the learned men known by the title of theologians of Holland, and even the great Newton, have added weight to the doctrine. These illustrious scholars imagine that neither Moses nor Joshua could write those books that are attributed to them: they say that their histories and laws would have been engraven upon wood, if in fact they had existed; that this art requires prodigious assiduity; and that it was not possible to cultivate this art in deserts. They found their opinion, as may be seen in other places, upon anticipation and apparent contradictions. In opposition to these great men, we embrace the common opinion, which is that of the synagogue and the church, whose infallibility we acknowledge.

Not that we dare accuse the Le Clercs, the Middletons, or the Newtons of impiety; God forbid! we are convinced that if the books of Moses and Joshua, and the rest of the Pentateuch, do not appear to them to come from the hands of those heroes of Israel, they were not less of opinion that these books were inspired. They acknowledge the finger of God in every line of Genesis, in Joshua, Sampson, and Ruth. The Jewish writer was, as we may say, nothing more than the secretary of God; that God who has dictated all things. Newton, doubtless could not think otherwise; this we sufficiently know. God keep us from resembling those perverse hypocrites, who avail themselves of every pretense to accuse all great men of irreligion, just as they were formerly accused of magic! We should think that we did not only act dishonestly, but cruelly insult the Christian religion, if we were so abandoned as to want to persuade the public, that the most learned men and the greatest geniuses upon earth are not true Christians. The more we respect that church which we submit to, the more we are of opinion that this church tolerates the opinions of these virtuous scholars, with that charity that forms its character.

XLI

OF THE JEWS AFTER MOSES, TILL THE TIME OF SAUL

I DO not endeavor to discover why Joshua or Josuah, captain of the Jews, in making his tribe pass from the east of Jordan to the west, towards Jericho, should want God to suspend the course of this river, which is not at that place forty feet wide, when it was so easy to throw a wooden bridge over, and when it was still more easy to ford it. There were several fords to this river, which is proved by the Israelites slaying at one of them the forty-two thousand Israelites, who could not pronounce the word *Shibboleth*.

I do not ask why Jericho should fall at the sound of trumpets; these are fresh prodigies, which God thought fit to operate in favor of the people whose king he had declared himself; this does not compose the spring of history. I shall not examine what right Joshua had to come and destroy villages, where his name had never been heard. The Jews said they were descended from Abraham; Abraham travelled among you about four hundred years ago, therefore your country belongs to us; and we ought to cut the throats of your mothers, wives, and children.

Fabricius and Holstenius have made the following objection. What should we say, if a Norwegian came into Germany with some hundreds of his countrymen, and told the

Germans that about four hundred years ago a countryman of ours, who was the son of a potter, travelled near Vienna; therefore Austria belongs to us, and we are come to sacrifice you all in the name of the Lord? The same authors consider that the time of Joshua is not ours; that it is not for us to cast a profane eye upon divine things; and particularly that God had a right to punish the sins of the Canaanites by the hands of the Jews.

We are told that no sooner was Jericho defenseless, than the Jews sacrificed to their God all the inhabitants, old men, wives, daughters, children sucking at the breast, and all the animals, except a female prostitute, who had concealed the Jewish spies in her house; spies that were besides useless, as the walls were to fall at the sound of trumpets. Why were all animals likewise killed, and might have been useful?

With respect to this woman, who in the Vulgate is called *Meretrix,* probably she afterwards led a more virtuous life, as she was David's grandmother. All these events are so many figures, or prophecies, which foretell from far the law of grace. Once more these are mysteries which we will not touch upon.

The book of Joshua relates that this chief, having made himself master of part of the country of Canaan, he hanged up thirty-one of its kings, that is, to say thirty kings and one of the principal burgesses, who had dared defend their fire-sides, their wives and children. We should here prostrate ourselves to providence, who chastised the sins of these kings by the sword of Joshua.

It is not at all astonishing that the neighboring people should unite against the Jews, who could appear as nothing

but an execrable banditti, to a people who were not enlightened, and not as the sacred instruments of divine vengeance,
and the future salvation of the human race. They were reduced to slavery by Cushan-rishathaim, king of Mesopotamia. It is true that Mesopotamia and Jericho are at a great
distance; Cushan-rishathaim must then have conquered Syria,
and part of Palestine. Be this as it may, they were in bondage
eight years, and remained afterwards sixty-two years upon
the same spot. These sixty-two years were a space of servitude, as they were commanded by the law to take all the
country from the Mediterranean to the Euphrates, all this
vast extent of country being promised* to them; and they
would doubtless have been tempted to seize upon it, if they
had been at liberty. They were eighteen years in bondage
under Eglon, king of the Moabites, who was assassinated by
Aod; they were afterwards for twenty-eight years slaves to
a people of Canaan, whom they do not name, till the warlike
prophetess Deborah delivered them. Gideon held them afterwards for seven years in bondage.

They were for eighteen years slaves to the Phenicians,
whom they call Philistines, till the time of Jephtha. They
were then for forty years more slaves to the Phenicians, till
the time of Saul. What may perplex our judgment is, that
they were slaves even in the time of Sampson, when Sampson
required only the jaw-bone of an ass to kill a thousand Philistines, and when God operated by the hands of Sampson
the most astonishing prodigies.

Let us stop a moment to observe, how many Jews were
exterminated by their own brothers, or by the order of God

* Genesis, chap. 15, v. 18. Deuter., chap. 1, v. 7.

himself, from the time that they wandered in the desert, till the time that they had a king elected by drawing lots.

The Levites, after the adoration of the golden calf, cast in a mold by Moses' brother, massacred 23,000 Jews.

Destroyed by fire, at Korah's revolt....250

Put to death for the same revolt 14,700

Put to death for having correspondence with Midianite girls 24,000

Slain at the ford of the Jordan, for not being able to pronounce the word Shibboleth...42,000

Killed by the tribe of Benjamin, who were attacked 40,000

Of the tribe of Benjamin, killed by the other tribes 45,000

When the ark was taken by the Philistines, and God to punish them, having afflicted them with the hemorrhoids, they brought back the ark to Bethsames, they offered the Lord five golden anuses, and five golden rats. The number of Bethsamites that were struck dead for looking at the ark was 50,070

Total number 239,020

Here are two hundred thirty-nine thousand and twenty Jews exterminated by the order of God himself, or by their civil wars, without reckoning those who perished in the Desert, or who died in the battles against the Canaanites, etc.

If we were to judge of the Jews as of other nations, we

could not conceive how the children of Jacob could have produced a race sufficiently numerous to sustain such a loss. But God who conducted them, God who tried them and punished them, rendered that nation so different from all the rest of men, that we should view them with other eyes than those with which we look upon the rest of the earth, and not judge of these events as we do of common events.

XLII

OF THE JEWS AFTER SAUL

THE JEWS do not appear to have enjoyed a happier lot under their kings than under their judges. Their first king, Saul, was obliged to put himself to death; Ishbosheth and Mephibosheth his sons were assassinated.

David delivered up seven grandsons of Saul to the Gabo-nites only to be perplexed. He ordered Solomon his son to put to death Adonijah his other son, and his general Joab. King Asa put part of the people in Jerusalem to death. Boasa assassinated Nadab, son to Jeroboam, and all his rela-tions. Jehu assassinated Joram and Josias, seventy sons of Ahab, forty-two brothers of the Acosias, and all their friends. Athaliah assassinated all her grandchildren, except Joash, and she is assassinated by the high-priest Jehoiada. Joash is assassinated by his servants. Amaziah is killed; Zacharias is assassinated by Sillum, who is assassinated by Manahem, which Manahem causes all pregnant women in Tapsa to have their bellies ripped up. Phaceia, son to Manahem, is assassinated by Oses, son to Ela. Manasses puts a great number of Jews to death, and the Jews assassinate Ammon, son to Manasses, etc.

In the midst of these massacres ten tribes, who are car-ried off by Salmanazar, king of the Babylonians, are enslaved and dispersed forever, except some husbandmen, who are kept to cultivate the land.

There still remain two tribes, who are soon enslaved in their turn for seventy years: at the expiration of these seventy years, the two tribes obtain permission from their conquerors and their masters, to return to Jerusalem. These two tribes, with the few Jews that may be remaining in Samaria, with the new foreign inhabitants, are all subjected to the kings of Persia.

When Alexander becomes master of Persia, Judea is comprised in his conquests. After Alexander, the Jews remain in subjection at one time to the Seleucids, his successors in Syria, and at another, to the Ptolemies, his successors in Egypt; constantly in subjection, and supporting themselves by no other means than carrying on the trade of brokers, as they did in Asia. They obtained some favors from Ptolemy Epiphanes, king of Egypt. A Jew named Joseph became farmer-general of the imposts in Lower Syria and Judea, which belonged to this same Ptolemy. This was the most fortunate state of the Jews; for it was at this time that they built the third part of their city, afterwards called the bosom of the Maccabees, because the Maccabees completed it.

From the yoke of king Ptolemy, they passed under that of Antiochus, the god-king of Syria. As they had enriched themselves in the farms, they became audacious, and revolted against their master Antiochus. The courage and great actions of the Maccabees at this period are celebrated by the Jews of Alexandria; but the Maccabees could not prevent the general Antiochus Eupator, son to Antiochus Epiphanes, from erasing the walls of the temple, leaving nothing but

188

the sanctuary subsisting, or the high-priest Onias, who was considered as the author of the revolt, from losing his head.

Never were the Jews more attached to their law than under the kings of Syria; they no longer adored foreign divinities; it was at this time that their religion was irrevocably fixed; and they were, nevertheless, more unhappy than ever, always in expectation of being delivered by the promises of their prophets, by the assistance of their gods, but abandoned by providence, whose decrees are unknown to man.

They had sometimes a breathing of tranquility by the intestine wars of the kings of Syria. But the Jews soon armed themselves one against another. As they had no kings, and as the first dignity was that of the sacrificing priest, violent parties arose, in order to obtain it; there was no method of obtaining the dignity of high-priest but by sword in hand, and the path to the sanctuary was strewed with his rivals' carcasses.

Hyrcan, of the race of the Maccabees, who was become high-priest, but still in subjection to the Syrians, caused David's sepulchre to be opened, in which the exaggerator Josephus pretends, that three thousand talents were found. This imaginary treasure should have been sought for, at the time of rebuilding the temple of Nehemiah. This Hyrcan obtained from Antiochus Sidetes the privilege of coining money. But as there never was any Jewish money, it is very probable that the treasure found in David's tomb was not very considerable.

It is remarkable that this high-priest Hyrcan was a Saducean, and that he neither believed in the immortality of the soul, nor in angels; a fresh subject of altercation, which began to divide the Saduceans and the Pharisees. These conspired against Hyrcan, and would have condemned him to be whipped and imprisoned. He avenged himself of them, and governed despotically.

His son Aristobulus was daring enough to create himself king during the troubles of Syria and Egypt. This was a more cruel tyrant than any who had oppressed the Jewish people. Aristobulus, who indeed prayed very regularly in the temple, and never ate any pork, starved his mother to death, and had his brother Antigonus slain. His successor was named John, or Johannes, who was as wicked as himself.

This Johannes, overwhelmed with crimes, left two sons, who waged war against each other. These two sons were Aristobulus and Hyrcan. The Romans then subdued Asia. Pompey as he passed by taught the Jews reason, took the temple, had the seditious hanged at the gates, and loaded the pretended king Aristobulus with irons.

This Aristobulus had a son, who was insolent enough to take upon himself the name of Alexander. He caused some emotions, he raised some troops, and finished his career by being hanged by order of Pompey.

At length, Mark Antony gave to the Jews for king an Idumean Arab of the country of those Amalekites so much cursed by the Jews. It was this same Herod, of whom St. Matthew relates, that he had all the little children put to death in the neighborhood of Bethlehem, upon being informed that a king of the Jews was born in that village; and that three Magi conducted by a star, came to offer him presents.

Thus were the Jews almost constantly subjugated or slaves. We know how they revolted against the Romans, and Titus had them all sold at market for the price of the animal of which they would not eat.

They met with a still more shocking fate under the emperors Trajan and Hadrian, and they deserved it. An earthquake happened in the time of Trajan, which swallowed up the finest cities of Syria. The Jews thought this was the signal of God's wrath against the Romans: they assembled, and armed themselves in Africa and in Cyprus: they were animated with such rage, that they devoured the limbs of the Romans, whom they had slain. But soon after, all the guilty were executed. Those who remained were animated with the same rage under Hadrian, when Barcochebas, who called himself their Messiah, headed them. This fanaticism was stifled by torrents of blood.

It is surprising that there should remain any Jews. The famous Benjamin of Tudel, a very learned rabbi, who travelled in Europe and Asia in the twelfth century, computed there were three hundred and eighty thousand Jews and Samaritans: for we must not mention the imaginary kingdom of Thema near Thibet, where this Benjamin, either deceived or deceiving, in this respect, asserts, that there were three hundred thousand Jews of the ancient tribes, assembled under one sovereign. The Jews never had any country to themselves since the time of Vespasian, except some hamlets of Arabia Felix towards the Red Sea. Mahomet was at first obliged to keep terms with them. But he, at length, destroyed the little dominion which they had established in the north of Mecca. It is from the time of Mahomet, that they have ceased to compose a body of people.

In pursuing simply the historical thread of the little Jewish nation, we see that they could have no other end. They boast of having issued from Egypt like a band of robbers, carrying away every thing they had borrowed from the Egyptians; they glory in having never spared either age, sex, or infancy, in the villages and boroughs they could seize upon. They have the effrontery to display an irreconcileable hatred against other nations; they revolt against all their masters; ever superstitious; ever envious of others' good; ever barbarous; abject in misfortunes, and insolent in prosperity. Such were the Jews in the opinion of the Greeks and Romans, who could read their books: but in the eyes of Christians, enlightened by the faith which they persecuted, they prepared the way for us. They have been the heralds of providence.

The other two nations, who are wandering like the Jews in the East, and who, like them, do not unite with any other people, are the Banians and the Parsis, called Guebres. These Banians, whose talent consists in trade, like the Jews, are the descendants of the first peaceable inhabitants of Judea; they have never mixed their blood with foreign blood, any more than the Brachmanes. The Parsis are those same Persians, who were formerly monarchs of the East, and sovereigns of the Jews. They have been dispersed since the time of Omur, and cultivate in peace part of the land where they reigned, faithful to that ancient religion of the Magi, adoring one only God, and preserving the sacred fire, which they look upon as the work and emblem of the Divinity.

I do not reckon those remains of the Egyptians, who adored the secrets of Isis, and who no longer subsist but in some vagabond troops, that will soon be eternally annihilated.

192

XLIII

OF THE JEWISH PROPHETS

WE WILL take care not to confound the Nabim and the Roheim of the Hebrews, with the impostures of the other nations. We know that God did not communicate himself to the Jews, except in some particular cases; as for example, when he inspired Balaam the prophet of Mesopotamia, and when he made him utter the contrary of what he was to have been made to say. This Balaam was the prophet of another God, and yet it is not said that he was a false prophet. We have already observed that the priests of Egypt were prophets and seers. What idea was affixed to this word? that of inspired. At one time the inspired divined the past, and sometimes the future: they often confined themselves to figurative expressions. Wherefore St. Paul quotes these verses of a Grecian poet, named Aratus: "All things live in God, all things move, all things breathe in God";* he calls his poet a prophet.

Were the title and quality of prophet dignities amongst the Hebrews, that is, a particular ministry legally fulfilled by certain chosen persons, in the manner of the Pythian dignity at Delphos? No; prophets were nothing more than such persons as felt themselves inspired, and to whom visions appeared. Hence it was that false prophets often rose without

* Acts of the Apostles, Chap. 17.

missions, who thought that they had the spirit of God, and who frequently occasioned great misfortunes, like the prophets of the Cevennes in the beginning of this century.

It was difficult to distinguish the false prophet from the true one. Wherefore Manasseh, King of Judea, had Isaiah sawn asunder. The king Sedecias could not decide between Jeremiah and Ananiah, who foretold contrary things; and he imprisoned Jeremiah. Ezekiel was slain by Jews his fellow captives. Micaiah having prophesied misfortunes to king Ahab and Josephat, another prophet, named Tsedekia, son to Cana, gave him a slap on the face, saying the spirit of the eternal has passed from my hand upon thy cheek. Ozeus, chap. ix declares that the prophets are fools, *stultum prophetam, insanum virum Spiritualam.* The prophets treated one another as visionaries and liars. There was no other method then of separating the true from the false but by waiting for the accomplishment of the predictions.

Elisha having repaired to Damascus in Syria, the king, who was sick, sent him forty camels laden with presents, to know if he should recover: Elisha replied, "that the king might recover, but that he would die." The king in fact died. If Elisha had not been a prophet of the true God, he might at all events have been suspected of equivocation; for if the king had not died, Elisha had foretold his curse, in saying he might recover, and as he had not specified the time of his death. But having confirmed his mission by striking miracles, his veracity could not be called in question.

We shall not here join with commentators in their endeavors to discover what was the double spirit that Elisha received from Elijah; nor the signification of the cloak which

194

Elijah gave him, in ascending to heaven in a car of fire drawn by flaming horses, such as are figured by the Greeks in poetry, when they represent the car of Apollo. We shall not fathom the type, what was the mystical sense of those forty-two little children, who upon seeing Elisha in the cross-way leading to Bethel, said to him in laughing, "Mount, bald-pate, mount"; and the prophet's vengeance thereupon, in calling forth two bears, who devoured the little innocents. The facts are known, and the sense may, perhaps, be latent.

An eastern custom should be noticed here, which the Jews carried to a surprising height. This usage was not only speaking in allegories, but expressing by singular actions things they wanted to signify. Nothing was then more natural than this custom; for men not having for any length of time written their thoughts except in hieroglyphics, they must have accustomed themselves to speak as they wrote.

Thus the Scythians (if Herodotus is to be credited) sent to Darah, whom we call Darius, a bird, a mouse, a frog, and five arrows; which signified that if Darius did not fly as swift as a bird, or if he did not hide himself like a mouse, or a frog, he would perish by their arrows. The story may not be true; but it is always a testimony of the emblems in use in those distant times.

Kings wrote in enigmas; we have examples of this in Hiram, in Solomon, and in the queen of Sheba. Tarquin the Proud, being consulted in his garden by his son, upon the proper method of behaving to the Gabians, answers only by beating down the poppies, which grew higher than the other flowers. By this he sufficiently expressed that the great should be exterminated, and the people spared.

To these hieroglyphics we may attribute fables, which were the first kind of writing amongst men. Fable is of a much more ancient date than simple history.

We must be a little familiarized with antiquity not to be scared at the actions and enigmatical discourses of the Jewish prophets.

Isaiah wants to acquaint king Achas, that he will in some years be delivered from the king of Syria, and the melk or petit king of Samaria united against him; he says to him, "Before a child is at age to discern good from evil, you will be delivered from these two kings. The lord will hire a razor to shave the head, the hair of the groin (which is signified by the feet), the beard, etc." Then the prophet takes two witnesses, Zachariah and Uriah; he lies with the prophetess; she brings forth a child, the Lord gives it the name of Maher-Salal-has-bas, "divide quickly the spoils:" and this signifies that the spoils of the enemies shall be divided.

I do not enter into the allegorical and infinitely respect-able sense which is given to this prophecy; I shall confine myself to the consideration of those customs which appear so extravagant to us at present.

The same Isaiah walks quite naked in Jerusalem, to sig-nify that the Egyptians shall be entirely stript by the king of Babylon.

What! will it be said is it possible that a man should walk quite naked in Jerusalem, without being taken notice of by justice? Yes, certainly; Diogenes was not the only one of antiquity who had this effrontery. Strabo in his fifteenth book, says there was a sect of Brachmanes in India, who would have been ashamed of wearing any clothing. We may still see penitents in India, who walk naked, loaded with chains, and an iron ring fixed to the *penis,* to expiate the crimes of the people. There are also some in Africa and in Turkey. These manners are not our manners; and I do not believe that in the time of Isaiah, there was a single custom that resembles any of ours.

Jeremiah was only fourteen years of age when he received the spirit. God stretched out his hand, and touched his mouth, because he had some difficulty in speaking. He immediately sees a boiling cauldron turned toward the north: this cauldron represents the people, who are to come from the North; and the boiling water signifies the misfortunes of Jerusalem.

He purchases a flaxen belt, puts it round his loins, and is going to hide it by God's order in a hole near the Euphrates. He afterwards returns for it, and finds it rotten. He explains to us himself the parable, saying, that the pride of Jerusalem shall rot.

He puts ropes round his neck, he loads himself with chains, he puts a yoke upon his shoulders; he sends these cords, chains, and yoke, to the neighboring kings, to direct them to submit to the king of Babylon, Nabuchodonosor, in whose favor he prophecies.

Ezekiel may surprise still more; he foretells to the Jews that the fathers will eat their children, and children will eat their fathers. But before this prediction is made, he sees four animals sparkling with light, and four wheels covered with eyes; he eats a volume of parchment; he is bound with chains. He draws a plan of Jerusalem upon a brick; he throws down an iron pan; he lies three hundred and ninety days upon the left side, and forty days upon the right side. He is to eat bread made of wheat, barley, beans, lentils, millet, and to cover it with human excrements. Thus, said he, will the children of Israel eat their bread besmeared with those nations among whom they shall be driven. But after having eaten this bread of sorrow, God allows him to cover it with only the excrement of oxen.

He cuts off his hair, and divides it into three parts; the first he puts into the fire, he cuts the second with a sword round the city, and disperses the other with the wind.

This same Ezekiel has still more surprising allegories.

He introduces the Lord, who speaks in this manner. "When thou wast born, thy navel-string was not cut, thou wast neither washed nor salted, thou hast become big; thy breast is formed, thy hair has appeared; I passed, I knew it was the time for lovers—I covered thee, and I stretched myself over thine ignominy—I gave thee covering for thy legs and feet, gowns of cotton, bracelets, necklace, and ear-rings—But fully confident of thy beauty, thou hast given thyself up to fornication—thou hast built a bad spot; thou hast prostituted thyself in the open ways; thou hast opened thy legs to every passenger—thou hast sought the most robust—courtesans receive money, and thou hast given money to thy lovers."

"Oolla* has committed fornication upon me, she hath been furiously enamored with her lovers, princes, magistrates, and cavaliers.—Her sister Ooliba hath prostituted herself with greater rage—Her luxury sought those who had the member of an ass, and who—like horses."

* Ezek., chap. xxiii.

198

These expressions appear to us very indecent and barbarous; they were not considered in this light among the
Jews; they signified the apostasies of Jerusalem and Samaria,
These apostasies were frequently represented as fornication
or adultery. Once more, we must not judge of the manners,
customs, and modes of expression of the ancients by our
own: they no more resemble each other than the French
language does the Chaldean and the Arabic.

The Lord, at first, orders the prophet Hosea, chap. i
to take for his wife a prostitute, and he obeys. This prostitute bears him a son. God calls this son Jezreel; this is a
type of the house of Jehu, which must perish, because Jehu
had killed Joram in Israel. The Lord afterwards commands
Hosea to wed an adulteress, who was beloved by another,
as the Lord loves the children of Israel, who pay respect to
foreign gods, and who love the skin of the grape, chap. iii.
The Lord in the prophecy of Amos threatens, that the cows
of Samaria, chap. iv shall be put into the cauldron. In a
word, every thing is opposite to our manners and the turn
of our minds, and if we examine the customs of all the Eastern
nations, we shall find them equally opposite to our usages,
not only in remote times, but even at present, when we are
better acquainted with them.

XLIV

OF THE PRAYERS OF THE JEWS

THERE ARE but few prayers of ancient people remaining. We have but two or three formularies of the mysteries, and the ancient prayer to Isis related in Apuleius. The Jews have preserved theirs.

If the character of a nation may be conjectured from the prayers which they offer up to God, we shall easily perceive that the Jews were a carnal and sanguinary people. They rather seem in their psalms to wish the death of the sinner than his conversion; and in the Eastern style, they require of God all terrestrial blessings.

"Thou shalt water the mountains, the earth shall be glutted with fruits.

"He causeth the grass to grow for the cattle, and herb for the service of man, that he may bring forth food out of the earth: and wine, that maketh glad the heart of man, and oil to make his face to shine.

"Judah is a kettle full of meat, the mount of the Lord is a congealed mount, a fat mountain: Why do you look upon the congealed mountains?"

But it must be acknowledged that the Jews cursed their enemies in a style no less figurative.

"Ask of me, and I shall give thee the heathen for thine

inheritance—and the uttermost parts of the earth for thy possession. Thou shalt break them with a rod of iron.

"Give them according to their deeds, and according to the wickedness of their endeavors: give them after the work of their hands, render to them their desert.

"Let the wicked be ashamed, and let them be silent in the grave.

"Take hold of the shield and buckler, and stand up for mine help. Draw out also the spear, and stop the way against them that persecute me—Let them be confounded and put to shame—Let them be as chaff before the wind—Let his net that he hath hid catch himself.

"Let death seize upon them, and let them go down quick into hell.

"Break their teeth, O God, in their mouth: break out the great teeth of the young lions, O Lord.

"Let them return, and let them make a noise like a dog —Let them wander up and down for meat, and grudge if they be not satisfied.

"Through God shall we do valiantly: for it is he that shall tread down our enemies.

"Rebuke the company of spearmen, the multitude of bulls, with the calves of the people; that thy foot may be dipped in the blood of thine enemies, and the tongue of thy dogs in the same.

"Pour out thine indignation upon them, and let thy wrathful anger take hold of them—Let their habitation be desolate, and let none dwell in their tents.

"Pour out thy wrath upon the heathen that have not known thee.

"Do unto them as unto the Midianites—O my God, make them like a wheel; as the stubble before the wind, as the fire burneth the wood.

"Set thou a wicked man to rule over him, and let Satan stand at his right hand; when he stall be judged, let him be condemned, and let his prayer become sin. Let his children be fatherless, and his wife a widow—Let his children be continually vagabonds, and let them beg. Let the extortioner catch all that he hath.

"The Lord is righteous, he hath cut asunder the cords of the wicked—Let them be as grass on the house tops.

"Happy shall he be that taketh and dasheth thy little ones against the stones."

We see that if God had granted all the prayers of his people, there had remained nothing but Jews upon earth; for they detested all nations, and they were detested by them; and by incessantly requiring God to exterminate all those whom they hated, they seemed to ask the destruction of the whole earth. But we should always remember, that the Jews were not only the cherished people of God, but the instruments of his vengeance. It was by them that he punished the sins of other nations, as he punished his people by these. It is no longer allowed to offer up the same prayers now, and request of him to let us rip up the bellies of mothers and those of children still sucking at the breast, and that they be dashed to pieces against the stones of the earth. God being acknowledged for the common father of all men, no one people make these imprecations against their neighbors. We have sometimes been as cruel as the Jews; but in singing their psalms, we do not turn the sense of them against the people who are at war with us. This is one of the great advantages of the law of forgiveness over the law of rigor; and would it had pleased God that under a holy law, and with divine prayers, we had not shed our brother's blood, and ravaged the earth in the name of a God of mercy!

XLV

OF JOSEPHUS, THE JEWISH HISTORIAN

WE SHOULD not be astonished that the history of Flavian Josephus should meet with antagonists, when it appeared at Rome. It is true there were but very few copies of it: an able copyist could not transcribe it in less than three months. The books were very dear and very scarce: few Romans deigned to read the Annals of an insignificant nation of slaves, whom the nobles and the plebeians equally despised. It nevertheless appears by Josephus's answer to Appion, that he met with a small number of readers; and we also find that this small number looked upon him as a liar and a visionary.

We should put ourselves in the place of the Romans in the time of Titus, to conceive with what contempt mixed with horror the conquerors of the known world, and the legislators of nations, must have looked upon the history of the Jewish people. These Romans could scarce know that Josephus had drawn the greatest part of his facts from the sacred books dictated by the Holy Ghost. They could not have been instructed that Josephus had added many things to the Bible, and had passed many over in silence. They were unacquainted that he had taken the foundation of some of his stories from the third book of Esdras; and that this book of Esdras is one of those that are called Apocryphal.

What must a Roman senator think in reading these Eastern tales? Josephus relates (book X, chap. xii) that Darius,
the son of Astyages, had appointed the prophet Daniel governor of three hundred and sixty cities, when he forbade,
upon pain of death, to pray to any God for a month. Certainly the scripture does not say that Daniel governed three
hundred and sixty cities.

Josephus seems to imagine afterwards that all the Persians
turned Jews.

The same Josephus gives the second temple of the Jews
rebuilt by Zorobabel a singular origin.

"Zorobabel," says he, "was the intimate friend of King
Darius." A Jewish slave an intimate friend of the king of
kings! this is much the same as if one of our historians should
tell us, that a fanatic of the Cevennes released from the galleys
was the intimate friend of Louis XIV.

Be this as it may, according to Flavian Josephus, Darius,
who was a very sensible prince, proposed to all his court
a question worthy of the *Mercure Gallant*,* namely which
had the most power, wine, kings, or women? The person
who gave the best answer was to be recompensed with a
flaxen head-dress, a purple robe, a golden necklace, to drink
out of a golden cup, lie in a golden bed, ride in a golden
chariot, drawn by horses with golden harnesses, and become
the king's cousin by patent.

Darius feted himself upon his golden throne to hear
the answers of his academy of wits. One entered into a dis-
sertation in favor of wine, another was for kings. Zorobabel
was an advocate for women. There is nothing so powerful

* A periodical publication.

as them; for I have seen, said he, Apamea, the mistress of the king my master, give his sacred majesty gentle slaps on the face, and take off his turban to dress her head with.

Darius found Zorobabel's answer so smart, that he immediately caused the temple of Jerusalem to be rebuilt.

This story is nearly similar to that which one of our most ingenious academics relates of Soliman and a turnup-nose, which has served for the ground-work of a very pretty burlesque opera. But we are compelled to acknowledge, that the author of the turnup-nose has not been gratified with either a golden bed, or a golden coach, and that the king of France has never called him cousin: we are no longer in the time of Darius.

These reveries, with which Josephus has crammed the holy books were doubtless, amongst the pagans, prejudicial to the facts which the Bible contains. The Romans could not distinguish between what had been drawn from an impure spring, and what Josephus had extracted from a pure spring. This sacred Bible, which we have, was either unknown to the Romans, or as much despised by them as Josephus himself. The whole was equally the object of raillery and that sovereign contempt which the readers conceived for the Jewish history. The apparitions of angels to the patriarchs, the passage of the Red Sea, the ten plagues of Egypt, the inconceivable multiplication of the Jewish people in so short a time, and in so circumscribed a spot; all the prodigies which signalized this unknown nation, were treated with that disdain which a people, conquerors of so many nations, a regal people, but to whom God had not divulged himself, naturally had for a little people reduced to slavery.

Josephus knew very well that all he wrote would be irreconcilable to profane writers: he says in several places, "the reader shall form what judgment he pleases of this." He is afraid of startling the minds of people; he diminishes as much as possible the faith that is due to miracles. We find he is every moment ashamed of being a Jew, at the very time he is exerting himself to make his nation appear amiable to their conquerors. The Romans, who were endowed with no other than common sense, and as yet had not faith, should doubtless be forgiven, for not considering the history of Josephus as any other than a miserable collection of ridiculous fables, related to them in order to extract some money from his masters. Bless God, we who have the happiness to be more enlightened than the Tituses, the Trajans, the Antoniuses, and the whole senate of Roman knights our masters; we, who are enlightened by superior luminaries, can distinguish between the absurd fables of Josephus, and the sublime truths that are declared to us by the holy scripture.

XLVI

OF A FALSEHOOD OF FLAVIAN JOSEPHUS, RELATING TO ALEXANDER AND THE JEWS

WHEN ALEXANDER, who was elected by all the Greeks like his father, (and as Agamemnon had formerly been) to go and avenge the injuries that Greece received from Asia, had gained the victory of Issus, he became master of Syria, one of the provinces belonging to Darah or Darius; he wanted to secure Egypt before he passed the Euphrates or the Tigris, and deprive Darius of all the posts by which he could be furnished with fleets. To compass this design, which was the plan of a very great captain, it was necessary to lay siege to Tyre. This city was under the protection of the kings of Persia, and was sovereign of the sea: Alexander took it, after an obstinate siege of seven months, in which he displayed as much art as courage; the dyke which he had the resolution to raise upon the sea coast is still looked upon as the model, which should be followed by all generals in similar enterprises. It was by imitating Alexander, that the duke of Parma took Antwerp, and cardinal Richelieu Rochelle, if it be allowed to compare small things with great. Rollin, indeed, says that Alexander took Tyre only because the inhabitants scoffed at the Jews, and that God would avenge the honor of his people. But Alexander might have had still other reasons; it was necessary, after having made

Tyre submit, not to lose a moment before he seized the post of Pelusium. So that Alexander having made a forced march to surprise Gaza, he went from Gaza to Pelusium in seven days. It is thus faithfully related by Arrian, Quintus Curtius, Diodorus, and even Paul Oroseus himself, according to the Journal of Alexander.

What doth Josephus to raise his nation in subjection to the Persians, fallen under the power of Alexander with all Syria, and afterwards honored with some privileges by this great man? He pretends that Alexander had, in a dream at Macedon, seen Jaddus the high-priest of the Jews (supposing there was a Jewish priest whose name terminated in *us*) that this priest had encouraged him to undertake his expedition against the Persians, and that this was the reason that Alexander had attacked Asia. He could not, then, avoid going six or seven days' march out of his way, after the siege of Tyre to visit Jerusalem. As the high-priest Jaddus had formerly appeared to Alexander in a dream, he received also in a dream an order from God to go and salute this king: he obeyed, and being dressed in his pontifical habit, followed by his Levites in surplices, he marched in procession before Alexander. As soon as this monarch saw Jaddus, he recollected the same man who had instructed him in a dream seven or eight years before, to come and conquer Persia; and this he told to Parmenio. Jaddus had upon his head his cap ornamented with a plate of gold, upon which a Hebrew word was engraven; Alexander, who was doubtless a proficient in Hebrew, immediately discovered the word Jehovah, and prostrated himself with humility, knowing very well that none but God could have this name. Jaddus instantly

209

displayed prophecies which clearly indicated that Alexander would conquer the empire of Persia; prophecies that were never made after the event had happened. He flattered Alexander, that God had chosen him to destroy all the hopes of his cherished people, to reign in the Land of Promise, in the same manner as he had formerly chosen Nabuchodonosor and Cyrus, who had successively possessed the Land of Promise. This absurd story of that romance-writer Josephus should not, methinks, have been copied by Rollin, as if it had been attested by a holy writer.

But in this manner has ancient history been written, and modern history often the same.

XLVII

OF POPULAR PREJUDICE TO WHICH THE SACRED
WRITERS HAVE DEIGNED TO CONFORM
THROUGH CONDESCENSION

THE HOLY books were made to teach morality and not physics.

The serpent was esteemed by antiquity as the most skilful of all animals. The author of the Pentateuch is pleased to say that the serpent was subtile enough to seduce Eve. Beasts were supposed sometimes to speak; the holy writer makes the serpent and Balaam's ass speak. Many Jews and many learned Christians have considered this history as an allegory; but whether it be emblematical or real, it is equally respectable. The stars were considered as points in the clouds: the divine author confines himself to this vulgar notion, and says, that the moon was created to preside over the stars.

The common opinion was, that the heavens were solid; they were called in Hebrew Rakiak, which word implies a plate of metal, a body extended and firm, which we translated into firmament. It contained waters, which were dispersed by openings. The scripture chimes in with this physical opinion.

The Indians, the Chaldeans, and the Persians, imagined that God had formed the world at six different times. The author of Genesis, not to startle the weakness of the Jews,

211

represents God as forming the world in six days; though a single word and a single instant would have been sufficient for his omnipotence. A garden and shade were looked upon as great blessings in a dry country, parched with the sun; the divine author places the first man in a garden.

They had no idea of a being purely immaterial. God is always represented as a man: he walks at noon in the garden, he speaks, and is spoken to.

The word Soul, Ruah, signifies breath, life; the soul is always used for life in the Pentateuch.

It was believed that there were nations of giants; and it is said in Genesis, that they were the children of angels and the daughters of men.

Brutes were granted a kind of reason. God, after the deluge, deigns to make alliance with brutes, the same as with men.

Nobody knew what the rainbow was; it was looked upon as something supernatural, and Homer always talks of it in this manner. The scripture calls it the ark of God, the sign of alliance.

Amongst many errors which mankind had adopted, it was believed that animals might be produced of any color that was desired, by showing those colors to the mothers before they conceived: the author of Genesis says, that Jacob had lambs spotted by this device.

All antiquity made use of charms against the bite of serpents; and when the wound was not mortal, or when it was happily sucked by quacks, called Psilles, or when some local application had been successfully made, it was never doubted but that the charms had operated. Moses erected a god, a brazen serpent, whose look cured those who had been bit with serpents. God turned a popular error into a new truth.

The notion that bees could be formed out of a rotten carcass was one of the most ancient errors. This idea was founded upon the daily experience of seeing flies and little worms covering the bodies of dead animals. From this experience, which deceived the eyes, all antiquity concluded that corruption was the principle of generation. As it was believed that a dead body produced flies, it was imagined that the certain method of procuring bees was to prepare the bleeding skins of animals in a proper manner, to operate this metamorphosis. It was not considered how great an aversion bees have for all corrupted flesh, and how very averse they are to all infection. The method of producing bees in this manner could not succeed: but this they attributed to an error in the preparation. Virgil, in his fourth book of the Georgics, says, "that this operation was successfully performed by Aristaeus"; but he also adds, that it "is a miracle," *mirabile monstrum.*

This ancient prejudice is rectified in relating that a hive of bees was found by Sampson in the jaws of a lion, which he had torn to pieces with his hands.

It was also a vulgar notion that the asp slit its ear for fear of hearing the voice of the enchanter. The Psalmist gives into this error, by saying, Ps. lviii "they are like the deaf adder, that stoppeth her ear; which will not hearken to the voice of charmers, charming never so wisely."

The ancient opinion that women who have their menses turn wine and milk, prevent butter from coagulating, and make young pigeons die in the dove-houses, still subsists with the vulgar, as well as lunar influences. It was thought that female purgation was the evacuation of corrupted blood; and that if a man approached his wife at that time, he would necessarily produce leprous and lame children. This notion so strongly prevented the Jews, that in the xxth chapter of Leviticus, the man and woman are both condemned to death, who perform conjugal duty at this critical time.

In fine, the Holy Spirit is so inclinable to conform to vulgar prejudices, that the Savior himself says, That new wine should never be put in old casks, and that the grain must rot to ripen.

St. Paul says to the Corinthians, in persuading them to believe a resurrection, "Thou fool, that which thou sowest is not quickened except it die." We know very well now, that the grain does not rot in the earth to grow; if it rotted it would not grow; but this error then prevailed: and the holy scriptures deigned to draw useful comparisons from it. This is what St. Jerome calls speaking economically.

All convulsive disorders were looked upon as possessions of the devil, as soon as the doctrine of devils was adopted. Amongst the Romans as well as the Greeks, the epilepsy was called the sacred disorder. Melancholy, attended with a kind of madness, was still a disorder, the cause of which was unknown; those who were seized with it ran barking about the tombs at night. They were called Demoniacs, and amongst the Greeks, Lykantropes. The scripture allows of demoniacs, who wander amongst the tombs.

Guilty people among the Greeks were frequently tormented by furies; they had reduced Orestes to such a state of despair, that he ate one of his fingers in one of his raving fits: they had haunted Alcmeon, Eteocles, and Polinices. The Hellenist Jews, who were instructed in all the Grecian opinions, at length admitted amongst them certain kinds of furies, foul fiends, devils who tormented men. It is true the Sadducees did not acknowledge devils; but the Pharisees received them a short time before the reign of Herod. There were at that time amongst the Jews exorcists, who drove out the devils; they made use of a root, which they put under the nose of the person possessed, and employed a formulary taken from a supposed book of Solomon. They were, at length, so skilful in the driving out devils, that our Saviour, who, according to St. Matthew, was himself accused of driving them out by the power of Beelzebub, grants the Jews the same power, and asks them if it is by means of Beelzebub that they triumph over evil spirits?

Certainly if the Jews, who put Jesus to death, had the power of performing such miracles; if the Pharisees in fact drove out devils, they performed the same prodigies as our Savior operated; they had the gift which Jesus communicated to his disciples; and if they had it not, Jesus conformed himself to the popular prejudices, in deigning to suppose that his implacable enemies, whom he called a race of vipers, had the gift of miracles, and prevailed over demons. It is true that neither the Jews nor the Christians any longer enjoy, at present, that prerogative which was for a length of time so common. There are always exorcists, but we no more meet with devils, or people possessed—so much do things change with time! It was then according to the order of things that people should be possessed; and it is proper there should be none in that situation at present. The necessary prodigies to raise a divine edifice are useless, when it has attained its utmost summit. Every thing on earth is changed; virtue alone never alters; it resembles the light of the sun, which contains scarce any known matter, and which is always pure, ever immutable, when all the elements are incessantly confounded. It is only necessary for us to open our eyes to bless its author.

XLVIII

OF ANGELS, GENII, AND DEVILS OF THE ANCIENT NATIONS, AND AMONGST THE JEWS

EVERY THING has its source in the nature of the human mind; all men in power, magistrates, and princes, had their messengers; it is probable, that the gods had also theirs. The Chaldeans and Persians seem to be the first people who mentioned angels. The Parsees, a religious sect that worshipped fire, and still subsist, communicated to the author of the religion of the ancient Parsees,* the names of the several angels which the primitive Parsees acknowledged. They amounted to an hundred and nineteen, amongst which we meet with neither the name of Raphael, nor that of Gabriel, the Parsees having adopted them long afterwards. The names are Chaldean, and were unknown to the Jews before their captivity; for before the history of Tobit, we do not meet with the name of any angel, either in the Pentateuch, or the other Hebrew books.

The Persians in their ancient catalogue prefixed to the Sadder, reckoned but twelve devils, of which Arimanes was the chief. It afforded them at least some consolation, to reflect that there were more good genii in the world than demons, the foes of mankind.

We do not find that this doctrine was followed by the

* Hyde, de religione veterum Persarum.

Egyptians. The Greeks, instead of tutelary genii, had their subordinate or secondary deities, their heroes, and demi-gods. Instead of devils, they had their Ates, Erinnis, and Eumenides. Plato, I think, was the first who spoke of a good and evil genius presiding over the actions of men. After him, both the Greeks and Romans piqued themselves upon each having his two genii; the evil one having more business and more success than his antagonist.

When the Jews had, at length, given names to their celestial militia, they divided them into ten distinct classes; namely, the saints, the rapid, the strong, the flames, the sparks, the deputies, the princes, the sons of princes, the images, the animated. But the muster-roll of this hierarchy is only to be found in the Talmud and the Targum, and not in the writings of the Hebrew canon.

These angels had constantly the human form, and thus are they still represented with the addition of wings. Raphael conducted Tobit. The angels that appeared to Abraham and to Lot eat and drank with these patriarchs; and the savage fury of the inhabitants of Sodom too strongly proves, that the angels of Lot were corporeal beings. It would, indeed, be difficult to comprehend how angels could have converted with men, and how these could have answered them, if they had not appeared in a human form.

The Jews had no other idea even of God. He speaks the human tongue with Adam and Eve; he even speaks to the serpent; he walks in the garden of Eden at mid-day. He deigned to converse with Abraham, with the patriarchs, and with Moses. There have been more commentators than one who have imagined that these words of Genesis, "let us make man like unto our image," should be understood literally; that the most perfect of earthly beings was a feeble resemblance of the form of his creator; and that this idea should induce men never to degenerate.

Though the form of the rebellious angels, and their transformation into demons, be the foundation both of the Jewish and Christian religion, it is remarkable that no mention is made of it either in Genesis, the books of the law, or in any other canonical writings. In Genesis, we are expressly told, that a serpent spoke to Eve, and seduced her. It is there also observed, that the serpent was the most cunning and subtle of all the beasts of the field; and we have before observed, that this was the opinion of all nations in regard to the serpent. It is farther positively asserted in Genesis, that the hatred of mankind towards the serpent arises from the ill office done by that creature to human kind: that from this time, it has endeavored to bite us, and we have endeavored to crush it; and that for its bad actions it is condemned in these words, "upon thy belly shalt thou go, and dust shalt thou eat all the days of thy life." It must be confessed, indeed, that serpents do not eat dust; but all the people of antiquity believed they did.

We are inclined to believe that occasion hath been taken from this representation to persuade mankind that this serpent was one of the rebellious angels transformed into demons, who came to avenge himself upon the works of God, and to corrupt them. There is not a single passage however in the Pentateuch from which we can make this inference, by the feeble light of human reason.

Satan appears, in Job, to be the master of the earth,

subordinate to God; but is there a man a little versed in antiquity, who knows not that Satan is a Chaldean word; that this Satan was the Arimanius of the Persians, adopted by the Chaldeans, the evil spirit that prevailed over man? Job is represented as an Arabian pastor, living upon the confines of Persia. We have already observed that the Arabian words retained in the Hebrew translation of this ancient allegory evince that the book was first written by the Arabians. Flavian Josephus, who does not include it among the writings of the Hebrew canon, removes all doubt upon this head.

Demons and devils, who were banished from a globe of heaven, precipitated into the center of our globe, and escaping from their prison to tempt mankind, have been considered for many ages as the authors of our damnation. But in this case, as in the former, this is an opinion of which no mention is made in the Old Testament. It is a traditional fact.

Some commentators have said, that this passage of Isaiah, "How hast thou fallen from the sky, O Lucifer, who didst appear in the morning?" implies the fall of the angels; and that it was Lucifer who disguised himself in the shape of a serpent to induce Eve and her husband, to eat the apple.

But in truth so foreign an allegory resembles those enigmas, which school-boys were formerly taught to believe. A picture, for example, was displayed of an old man and a young woman. One said this was winter and spring; another snow and fire; another a rose and a thorn, or strength and weakness: and he who solved it the most foreign to the purpose, who gave the most extraordinary explanation, gained the prize.

It is precisely the same with regard to the singular appli- cation of the morning-star to the devil. Isaiah, chap. xiv insulting the death of a king of Babylon, says to him, "The whole earth is at rest, and is quiet; they break forth in re- joicing and singing. Yea, the fir trees rejoice at thee; and the cedars of Lebanon, saying, Since thou art laid down no feller is come amongst us. Thy pomp is brought down to the grave, and the noise of the viols: the worm is spread under thee, and the worms cover thee. How art thou fallen from heaven, O Lucifer (Helel), son of the morning? how art thou cut down to the ground, which didst weaken the nations?"

This Helel is translated into Latin by the word Lucifer; and this name has been since given to the devil, though there certainly is very little connection between the devil and the morning-star. It has been imagined that this devil, being a star fallen from heaven, was an angel who had waged war against God; he could not do it alone, he must there- fore have had accomplices. The fable of the giants armed against the gods, and who were spread through every nation, is, according to many commentators, a profane imitation of the tradition, which teaches us that angels had risen against their masters. This notion received fresh strength from the epistle of St. Jude, where it is said, "And the angels, which kept not their first estate, but left their own habitation, he hath reserved in everlasting chains under darkness, unto the judgment of the great day. Woe unto them, for they have gone in the way of Cain, and Enoch also, the seventh from Adam, prophesied of these, saying, Behold, the lord cometh with ten thousands of his saints, etc."

It has been imagined by some, that Enoch left a written history of the fallen angels. But to this there are two objec' tions. In the first place, Enoch wrote as little as Seth, to whom, nevertheless, the Jews impute some writings: and as to the false Enoch, cited by St. Jude, his testimony is acknowl' edged to be forged by a Jew.* Secondly, this false Enoch says not a word of the rebellion or fall of the angels before the formation of man. He says word for word in his *Egre' gori*, or, as they are styled in our version, the "sons of God."

"The number of men being prodigiously increased, they had very handsome daughters; the angels watching over them, *Egregori*, became enamored, and were led into many errors. They were provoked, and said among themselves, let us choose wives for ourselves amongst the daughters of the men of the earth. Semianas, their prince, said, I am afraid that you dare not accomplish such a design, and that I alone shall be answerable for the crime. They all replied, let us vow to execute our design, and let us be anathematized, if we fail. They united themselves then by oath, and uttered imprecations. They were two hundred in number. They sat out together in the time of Jared, and went upon the moun'

* This Book of Enoch must nevertheless be of some antiquity; for we find it frequently quoted in the Testament of the twelve Patriarchs, another Jewish book corrected by a Christian of the first century; and this Testament of the twelve Patriarchs is even quoted by St. Paul in his first epistle to the Thessalonians, if repeating the page word for word can be called quoting it. In the sixth chapter of the Patriarch Reuben, we find, "The scholar of God at length fell upon them," which St. Paul says verbatim. These twelve Testa' ments are not in other respects entirely conformable to Genesis. The incest of Juda, for example, is not related in the same manner. Juda says, that being drunk, he abused his daughter-in-law. The testament of Juda is remarkable in this respect, that it allows of seven organs of sense in man, instead of five; he reckons life and the act of generation as two senses. Moreover, all these patriarchs repent, in this Testament, having sold their brother Joseph.

tains called Hermonim, on account of their oath. The names of their chiefs were, Semiaxas, Atarculph, Araciel, Chobabiel Hosampsich, Zaciel Parmar, Thousael, Samiel, Tiril, Sumiel.

"These and the rest took women unto them, in the year eleven hundred and seventy of the creation of the world. From this commerce sprung three generations of men, the giants Naphilim, etc."

The author of this fragment writes in a style, which seems to belong to the primitive times; it carries with it the same simplicity. He names the personages, and does not forget the dates; but without either reflections or maxims: this is the ancient oriental manner.

We see that this story is founded on Genesis, chap. vi. "There were giants in the earth in those days; and even after that when the sons of God came in unto the daughters of men, and they bore children to them; the same became mighty men, which were of old men of renown."

Both the book of Enoch and Genesis perfectly agree, in regard to the copulation of these angels, or sons of God, with the daughters of men, and also as to the race of giants, their issue. But neither this book of Enoch, nor any one of the Old Testament, mentions a syllable of the war of the angels against God, their defeat, their descent into hell, nor of their enmity to mankind.

No mention is made of evil spirits, or the devil, but in the allegory of Job, which we have spoken of, and which is not a Jewish book; and in the adventure of Tobit. The devil Asmodea, or Shammadey, who killed the first seven husbands of Sarah, and whom Raphael dislodged with the smoke of a fish's liver, was not a Jew devil, but a Persian. Raphael went and chained him in Upper Egypt; but it is certain, that the Jews having no idea of hell, they could not have any of devils. They began, very late, to believe in a hell and the immortality of the soul; and this was not till the sect of the Pharisees prevailed. They were, therefore, very far from thinking the serpent which tempted Eve was a devil, or fallen angel, precipitated into hell. This opinion, which serves as the foundation-stone of the whole edifice, was laid down last of all. Not that we have the less reverence for the history of the fallen angels; but we know not whence to deduce its origin.

Beelzebub, Belphegor, and Astorath, were called devils; but these were ancient gods of Syria. Belphegor was the god who presided over marriage; Beelzebub, or Bel-se-buth, sig-nified the Lord who preserved insects. Even king Okosias had consulted him as a god, to know if he would be cured of a disorder; and Elijah, who was affronted at this step, said, "Is there no God in Israel, that the God of the Alcoran must be consulted?"

Astorath signified the moon, and the moon did not ex-pect to be transformed into a devil.

The apostle Jude says again, "that the devil quarreled with the angel Michael about the body of Moses." But we find nothing similar to this in the Jewish canons. This dispute of Michael with the devil, is only in an apocryphal book, entitled the *Analysis of Moses,* quoted by Origen in the third Book of his Principii.

It is therefore certain, that the Jews acknowledged no devils, till about the time of their captivity in Babylon. They borrowed this doctrine from the Persians, who had it from Zoroaster.

These facts cannot be disputed, except by ignorance, fanaticism, or want of candor; and we should add, that religion has nothing to dread from the consequences. God certainly allowed the belief of good and evil genii, of the immortality of the soul, and of eternal rewards and punishments, to be received by twenty different nations before it reached the Jews. Our holy religion has consecrated those doctrines; it has established what the others had only a glimpse of; and that which among the ancients was nothing more than an opinion, has become by revelation one of the divine truths.

XLIX

WHETHER THE JEWS TAUGHT OTHER NATIONS, OR WHETHER THEY WERE TAUGHT BY THEM

HOLY WRIT having never determined whether the Jews were the masters or the disciples of other nations, it is allow-able to examine the question.

Philo, in the account he gives of his mission to Caligula, begins by saying that Israel is a Chaldean word; that it was a name the Chaldean gave to the just who were consecrated to God; that Israel signified seeing God. This alone seems to prove, that the Jews did not call Jacob Israel; that they did not take upon themselves the names of Israelites, till such time as they had some knowledge of this Chaldean tongue. Now they could have no knowledge of this tongue but when they were slaves in Chaldea. Is it probable that they had already learned in the deserts of Arabia Petraea the Chaldean language?

Flavian Josephus in his reply to Appion, Lysimachus, and Molon (book II, chap. v) plainly acknowledges, "that the Egyptians taught other nations circumcision, as Herodotus testifies." And would it really be probable that the ancient and powerful nation of the Egyptians should have adopted this custom from a little people, whom they abhorred, and who, according to their own account, did not practice circum-cision till the time of Joshua?

The sacred books themselves teach us that Moses was brought up in the Egyptian sciences; and they nowhere say that the Egyptians ever learned anything from the Jews. When Solomon wanted to build his temple and his palace, did he not desire the king of Tyre to send him workmen? It is even said that he gave twenty cities to the king of Hiram to obtain workmen and cedar: this was doubtless paying very dear, and the bargain was very strange; but did the Tyrians ever ask any artists of the Jews?

The same Josephus whom we have mentioned, acknowledges that his nation, which he strives to raise, "had not for a long time any commerce with other nations"; that it was "particularly unknown to the Greeks, who were acquainted with the Scythians and the Tartars. Is it surprising," he adds book I, chap. v, "that our nation distant from the sea, and not piquing themselves upon having written anything, should be so little known?"

When the same Josephus relates with his usual exaggerations, the manner equally honorable as incredible, in which the king Ptolemy Philadelphus purchased a Greek translation of the Jewish books, done by Hebrew writers in the city of Alexandria; Josephus, I say, adds that Demetrius of Pharlereus, who ordered this translation for his king's library, asked one of the translators how it happened that no historian, no foreign poet, had ever spoke of the Jewish books? The translator replied, "As these laws are all divine, no one has dared to undertake speaking of them, and those who have thought proper to do it, have been chastised by God." Theopompus, being inclined to insert some part of it in his history, lost his senses for thirty years; but being acquainted

227

in a dream, that he had become an idiot for wanting to pene-
trate into divine things, and acquaint the profane* therewith, he appeased the wrath of God by prayers, and recovered
his senses.

"Theodectes, a Grecian poet, having introduced some
passages, which he had taken from our holy books, in a
tragedy, immediately became blind; and did not recover his
sight till after he had acknowledged his fault."

These two stories of Josephus, which are unworthy of
a place in history, or of being related by a man that has
common sense, are in fact contradictory to the praises he
bestows upon this Greek translation of the Jewish books;
for if it was a crime to insert any part of them in another
language, it was, doubtless, a far greater crime to enable all
the Greeks to understand them. Josephus, in relating these
tales, at least agrees that the Greeks never had any knowledge of the writings of his nation.

On the contrary, as soon as the Hebrews were established
in Alexandria, they studied Grecian literature; they were
called the Hellenist Jews. It is therefore doubtless, that the
Jews from the time of Alexander learned many things from
the Greeks, whose language was become that of Asia Minor,
and of part of Egypt; and that the Greeks could acquire
nothing from the Hebrews.

* Joseph. Hist. of the Jews, book XII. Chap. xii.

L

OF THE ROMANS; THE BEGINNING OF THEIR EMPIRE AND THEIR RELIGION; THEIR TOLERATION

THE ROMANS cannot be reckoned amongst the primitive nations. Rome has existed only seven hundred and fifty years before our vulgar era. When they had rites and laws, they adopted them from the Tuscans and the Greeks. The Tuscans communicated to them the superstition of augurs; a super-stition, nevertheless, founded upon physical observations; upon the passage of birds, from whence they foretold the change of the atmosphere. It appears that all superstition hath something natural for its principle, and that many errors are derived from truth that is abused.

The Greeks furnished the Romans with the law of the twelve tables. A people who apply to another nation for laws and gods, must be a small and barbarous people: and such were the first Romans. Their territory in the time of the kings and the first consuls were not so extensive as those of Ragusa. We must not by this title of king, understand a monarch such as Cyrus, and his successors. The chief of a little people living by rapine can never be despotic. The spoils are divided in common, and each one defends his lib-erty as his own property. The first kings of Rome were the captains of freebooters.

If we are to credit the Roman historians, this little people began by ravishing the girls, and seizing upon their neighbors' goods. They should have been exterminated; but the ferocity and want which led them on to rapine, crowned their unjust enterprises with success; they maintained themselves, by being always at war; and at length, after about four centuries had elapsed, being more warlike than any other people, they made them all submit one after the other, from the extremity of the Adriatic gulf to the Euphrates.

In the midst of rapine, the love of their country always predominated, till the time of Sylla. This love of their country consisted for upwards of four hundred years in bringing something to the common stock of what had been pillaged from other nations. This is the virtue of robbers. Patriotism is murdering and fleecing other men. But great virtues existed in the heart of the republic. The Romans polished by time, polished all the barbarians they conquered, and became at length the legislators of the West.

The Greeks appeared in the early times of their republic, as a nation superior to the Romans. These do not issue from the haunts of their seven mountains with a handful of hay (*manipli*) which serve them for standards, only to sack the neighboring villages. They, on the contrary, are employed only in defense of their liberty. The Romans rob four or five hundred miles in circumference, the Equi, the Volsci, and the Antiates. The Greeks repulse the innumerable armies of the great king of Persia, and triumph over him by land and sea. The victorious Greeks cultivate and improve all the fine arts; and the Romans are entirely ignorant of them, till about the time of Scipio Africanus.

I shall make two important observations here with respect to their religion; the first is they adopted or allowed the doctrine of every other people, after the example of the Greeks; and that in reality the senate and the emperors always acknowledged one supreme God, as well as the greatest part of the philosophers and poets of Greece.

The toleration of all religions was a natural law, engraven in the hearts of all men. For what right can one created being have to compel another to think as he does? but when a people are united, when religion is become a law of the state, we should submit to that law. Now, the Romans by their law adopted all the Gods of the Greeks, who themselves had altars for the gods unknown, as we have already observed.

The twelve tables ordained, *separatim nemo habessit deos neve advenas nisi publice adscitos,* "That no one should have foreign or new gods without the public sanction." This sanction was given to many doctrines; and all the others were tolerated. This association of all the divinities of the world, this kind of divine hospitality, was the law of nations from all antiquity, except one or two little nations.

As there were no dogmas, there was no religious war. It was enough that ambition and rapine should shed human blood, without religion accomplishing the extermination of the world.

It is also very remarkable that amongst the Romans no one was ever persecuted for his way of thinking. There is not a single example from the time of Romulus down to Domitian; and amongst the Greeks, Socrates is the only exception.

It is again incontestable that the Romans, as well as the

Greeks, adored one supreme God. Their Jupiter was the only god who was looked upon as the master of thunder, the only one that was styled the most great and the most good God, *Deus optimus maximus*. Thus from Italy to India and China, you find the doctrine of one supreme God, and the toleration in all nations that were known.

With this knowledge of one God, with this universal indulgence, which are everywhere the fruit of cultivated reason, were blended innumerable superstitions, which were the ancient fruits of reason erroneous and in its dawn. We know that the sacred fowls, the goddess Pertunda, and the goddess Cloacina, are ridiculous.

Why did not the conquerors and legislators of so many nations abolish such nonsense? Because being ancient, it was dear to the people, and was no way prejudicial to the govern- ment. The Scipios, the Paulus Emiliuses, the Ciceros, the Catos, the Caesars, had other employment than that of com- bating popular superstition. When an ancient error is estab- lished, policy avails itself of it, as a bit which the vulgar have put into their own mouth, till such time as another superstition arises to destroy it, and policy profits of this second error as it did of the first.

LI

QUESTIONS UPON THE CONQUESTS OF THE ROMANS, AND THEIR DECAY

HOW HAPPENED it that the Romans, who consisted of only three thousand people, and who possessed nothing more than a borough of about a thousand paces in circumference under Romulus, in time became the greatest conquerors of the earth? and whence arose that the Jews, who pretend to have had six hundred thirty thousand soldiers upon coming out of Egypt, who were surrounded with miracles, who fought under the God of armies, could never conquer Tyre and Sidon in their neighborhood? could never be ready to attack them? Why were those Jews almost continually in a state of slavery? They possessed all the enthusiasm and all the ferocity necessary for conquerors; the God of armies was always at their head; and yet the Romans, who were one thousand eight hundred miles distant from them, at length came to conquer them, and sell them at market.

Is it not evident (humanly speaking, and without considering secondary causes) that if the Jews, who were in hopes to conquer the world, were almost constantly in a state of servitude, it was their own fault? And if the Romans ruled, did they not deserve it by their courage and their prudence? I most humbly beg pardon of the Romans for comparing them one instant to the Jews.

How came it that the Romans, for upwards of four hundred and fifty years, could conquer only an extent of country of about twenty-five leagues? Was it not because their number was very small, and that the adversaries, whom they constantly had to combat with, were not more numerous than themselves? But having at length incorporated with themselves their conquered neighbors, their forces were sufficient to oppose Pyrrhus.

All the little nations that surrounded them being then become Romans, they composed a people entirely warlike, sufficiently formidable to destroy Carthage.

Why were the Romans employed seven hundred years to obtain at length an empire about as extensive as that which Alexander conquered in seven or eight years? Was it because they had always warlike nations to oppose, and that Alexander had to do with an effeminate people?

How came the empire to be destroyed by barbarians? Were not these barbarians more robust and greater warriors than the Romans, enervated in turn under Honorius and his successors? When the Cimbri came and threatened Italy in the time of Marius, the Romans ought to have foreseen that the Cimbri, that is to say, the people of the North, would destroy the empire when Marius was no more.

The weakness of the emperors, the factions of their ministers and their eunuchs, the enmity which the ancient religion of the empire excited against the new one, the bloody quarrels that arose in Christendom, theological disputes left to the management of arms, and effeminacy to valor, multitudes of monks replacing husbandmen and soldiers; everything tended to introduce these barbarians, who could not have

234

conquered the warlike republic, and who overwhelmed Rome languishing under cruel emperors and voluptuous devotees.

When the Goths, the Heruli, the Vandals, and the Huns, overspread the Roman empire, what measures did the two emperors take to stop the torrent? The difference between *Omoosios* and *Omousios* had thrown all the East and West into confusion. Theological persecutions completed the destruction of every thing. Nestorius, patriarch of Constantinople, who at first gained great credit under Theodosius II prevailed upon the emperor to persecute those who thought the penitent Christian apostates should be rebaptised; those who thought that Easter should be celebrated the fourteenth moon of March, those who did not dip the baptized three times. In a word, he so much tormented the Christians, that they in turn tormented him. He called the holy Virgin, Antropotokos; his adversaries, who wanted to have her called Theotokos, and who, doubtless, were right, since the council of Ephesus decided it in their favor, commenced a violent persecution against them. These disputes engaged every one's attention: and whilst they were thus employed, the barbarians divided amongst them Europe and Africa.

But why did not Alaric, who in the beginning of the fifth century marched from the banks of the Danube towards Rome, begin by attacking Constantinople, when he was master of Thrace? Why did he risk being cramped between the eastern and western empires? Is it natural that he should want to pass the Alps and Apennine mountains, when trembling Constantinople offered itself for conquest? The historians of those times, as badly instructed as the people were ill-governed, do not unravel this mystery; but it is easy to form a conjecture thereupon. Alaric had been general in the armies of Theodosius II a violent prince, an imprudent devotee, who lost the empire by entrusting the Goths with its defense. He conquered with them Eugenius his competitor; but the Goths thereby learned that they could gain victories for themselves. Alaric and the Goths were mercenaries to Theodosius. The pay they received became a tribute, when Arcadius, the son of Theodosius, was upon the throne of the East. Alaric therefore spared his tributary, to fall upon Honorius and upon Rome.

Honorius's general was the celebrated Stilicon, the only one that could defend Italy, and who had already stopped the progress of the barbarians. Honorius had him beheaded upon a mere suspicion, without any kind of trial. It was more easy to assassinate Stilicon than to defeat Alaric. This unworthy emperor, being retired to Ravenna, left the barbarian, who was his superior in every thing, to lay siege to Rome. The ancient mistress of the world saved herself from pillage at the price of five thousand pounds weight of gold, thirty thousand of silver, four thousand robes of silk, three thousand of purple, and three thousand pounds of spice. The money of India paid the ransom for Rome.

Honorius would not abide by the treaty. He sent some troops, who were destroyed by Alaric. He entered Rome in 409; and a Goth there created an emperor, who became his first subject. The year after, being deceived by Honorius, he punished him in sacking Rome. Then all the western empire was rent; the inhabitants of the North made incursions

on every side, and the emperors of the East could not maintain themselves but by becoming tributary.

In this manner Theodosius II paid tribute to Attila.
Italy, Gaul, Spain, and Africa, became the prey of every
assailant. This was the fruit of Constantine's unnatural policy, who had transferred the Roman empire into Thrace.

Is there not some visible destiny in the prosperity or
destruction of states? He that should have foretold Augustus,
that the Capitol would be one day possessed by the priest
of a religion derived from that of the Jews, would have
greatly astonished Augustus. Why did this priest afterwards
seize upon the city of the Ciceros and Caesars? Because he
found it in a state of anarchy. He became master of it, without making scarce any effort, as the German bishops about
the thirteenth century became the sovereigns of those whom
they served as pastors.

Every event produces another that was unexpected.
Romulus did not imagine he should lay the foundation of
Rome for Gothic princes or bishops. Alexander did not sus-
pect that Alexandria would ever belong to the Turks; and
Constantine did not raise Constantinople for Mahomet II.

LII

OF THE PEOPLE WHO WROTE HISTORY, AND OF THE FABLES OF THE FIRST HISTORIANS

IT IS incontestable that the most ancient annals of the world are those of China. In these annals there is no uninterrupted succession, circumstantial, complete, judicious, without any mixture of the marvellous, and all supported by astronomical observations, for four thousand one hundred and fifty-two years. They recur to many more distant ages, without indeed any precise date, but with that probability which seems to approach certainty. It is very likely that powerful nations, such as the Indians, the Egyptians, the Chaldeans, the Syrians, who had great cities, had also annals.

The wandering people must have been the last who wrote, having less means of procuring and preserving archives, having few wants, few laws, few events, being occupied with nothing but the method of procuring a precarious subsistence, and being satisfied with oral tradition. A hamlet had never any history, a wandering people still less, and a single city very rarely.

The history of a nation cannot be written till very late; it is begun by some summary registers, which are preserved, as far as they can be, in a temple or citadel. An unhappy war often destroys these annals, and the people must renew their labors twenty times, like ants whose habitations are trampled upon; many ages must elapse before a history any way circumstantial can succeed to these indigested registers; and this first history is constantly mingled with marvellous errors, to supply the place of truth that is deficient. Thus the Greeks had not their Herodotus, till the eightieth Olympiad, upwards of a thousand years after the epocha inscribed upon the marbles of Paros. Fabius Pector, the most ancient historian amongst the Romans, did not write till the time of the second Carthaginian war, about five hundred and forty years after the foundation of Rome.

Now, if these two nations, the most lively upon earth, the Greeks and Romans, our masters, so late began their history, if our northern nations had no historian before Gregory of Tours, can we sincerely believe that the vagabond Tartars, who sleep upon snow, or the Troglodites, who hide themselves in caverns, or wandering Arabian robbers, who rove upon sandy mountains, had any Thucydideses, any Xenophons? Could they know any thing of their ancestors? Could they gain any knowledge before they had any cities, before they inhabited them, before they had summoned thither all the arts of which they were deprived?

If the Samoiedes, or the Nazamons, or the Esquimaux, should come and produce antedated annals many centuries back, replete with astonishing feats of arms, and a continued series of prodigies, which astonish nature, should we not laugh at these poor savages? And if some people, fond of the marvellous, or interested in making it credited, should torture their imagination to render these follies probable, should we not deride their attempts? and if they should add to this absurdity the insolence of affecting to hold the learned

239

in contempt, and the cruelty of persecuting those who doubted, would they not be the most execrable of men? Let a Siamese come and relate to me the metamorphoses of Samonocodom, and threaten to burn me if I offer any objections, how should I behave to this Siamese?

The Roman historians relate to us, indeed, that the god Mars had two children by a vestal, in an age that there were no vestals in Italy; that a she-wolf nourished these children, instead of devouring them, as we have already seen; that Castor and Pollux fought for the Romans; that Curtius cast himself into a gulf, and that the gulf closed up; but the Roman senate never condemned to death those who doubted of these prodigies: they were allowed to be laughed at in the Capitol.

There are in the Roman history very possible events that are not very probable. Many learned men have already called in question the adventure of the geese that saved Rome, and that of Camillus, who entirely destroyed the army of the Gauls. The victory of Camillus is, indeed, very brilliant in Titus Livius; but Polybius, who was earlier than Titus Livius, and more a statesman, says precisely the contrary: he assures us, that the Gauls, fearing to be attacked by the Veneti, departed from Rome loaded with booty, after having made peace with the Romans. Which shall we credit, Titus Livius or Polybius? we will at least remain in doubt.

Must we not doubt again the punishment inflicted upon Regulus, who is closed in a box stuck round with iron spikes? This kind of death is certainly without example. Would this same Polybius, who was almost his contemporary, Polybius who was upon the spot, and who has written in so superior

240

a manner the Roman and Carthaginian war, have passed over in silence so extraordinary and important a fact, and which would have so completely justified the insincerity of the Romans toward the Carthaginians? How would this people have dared so barbarously to have violated the law of nations with Regulus, at a time that the Romans had in their hands several of the chief citizens of Carthage, upon whom they might have revenged themselves?

In short, Diodorus Siculus relates, in one of his fragments, that the children of Regulus, having very ill treated some of the Carthaginian prisoners, the senate of Rome reprimanded them, and paid respect to the law of nations. Would they not have allowed a just revenge to the children of Regulus, if their father had been assassinated at Carthage? The history of Regulus's punishment gained credit in time; the enmity that subsisted between Rome and Carthage made it current; Horace sung it, and it was no longer doubted.

If we cast our eyes upon the primitive times of our history of France, everything is, perhaps, as false as it is obscure and disgusting; it is, at least, very difficult to believe the adventure of one Childeric, and one Bazine, the wife of Bazin, and of a Roman captain elected king of the Franks, who had hitherto no kings.

Gregory of Tours is our Herodotus, with this difference, that this inhabitant of Tours is not so amusing or so elegant as the Grecian. The monks, who wrote after Gregory, had they more understanding or veracity? were they not sometimes profuse of extravagant praise to assassins who had given them lands? did they never calumniate wise princes who gave them nothing?

I know very well that the Franks, who invaded Gaul, were more cruel than the Lombards who seized upon Italy, or the Visigoths who reigned in Spain. We meet with as many murders, and as many assassinations in the annals of the Clovises, the Thierres, the Childeberts, the Chilperics, and the Clotariuses, as in those of the kings of Judea and Israel. Nothing certainly could be more brutal than those barbarous times; nevertheless, is it not allowable to doubt of the execution of queen Brunehaut?

She was near eighty years of age, when she died in 613 or 614. Fredegaire, who wrote towards the end of the eighth century, one hundred and fifty years after the death of Brune-haut (and not in the seventh century, as we find it by an error of the press in the Chronological Abridgment) Frede-gaire, I say, assures us that Clotarius, a very pious prince, greatly fearing God, humane, patient, and meek, made queen Brunehaut ride round his camp upon a camel, and afterwards had her tied by the hair, an arm and one leg, to the tail of a vicious mare, which dragged her violently along the ground, broke her head upon the flint stones, and tore her to pieces, after which she was burnt to ashes. The camel, the vicious mare, a queen eighty years of age, tied by the hair and a foot to the mare's tail, are not things that frequently occur.

It would perhaps be difficult to fasten a woman of that age by her head of hair, it being so thin, to a horse's tail; and to tie her at the same time by the hair and a foot. And whence arose the pious design of burying Brunehaut in a tomb at Autun, after having burnt her in a camp? The monks Fredegaire and Aimoin assert it; but were these monks de Thous and Humes?

There was another monument erected for this queen in the thirteenth century in the abbey of St. Martin d'Autun, which she had founded. In this sepulchre was found the fragment of a spur. This spur it is said was used upon the vicious mare. It is a pity that the skin of the camel, which the queen mounted, was not also found. Is it not possible that this spur came there accidentally, or rather to do her honor? For in the fifteenth century a gilt spur was a great mark of honor. In a word, is it not reasonable for us to suspend our judgment upon this strange adventure so badly authenticated? It is true, that Paquier says the death of Brunehaut "was foretold by the Sybil."

All the barbarous ages are ages of horror and miracles. But is all that the monks have written to be believed? They were almost the only people who knew how to read and write, when Charlemagne did not know how to sign his name. They have acquainted us with the dates of some great events. We believe with them that Charles Martel defeated the Saracens; but that he killed three hundred and sixty-nine thousand in battle, is saying a great deal.

They say that Clovis, the second of that name, became an idiot; the thing is not impossible: but that God afflicted his brain, to punish him for having taken an arm of St. Denis in the church of those monks to place in his oratory, is not so probable.

If there were no other than such like stories to be erased from the history of France, or rather the history of the kings of the Franks and their mayors, we might prevail upon ourselves to read it. But how can we endure the barbarous lies with which it is replete? Villages and fortresses that never existed are continually besieged. There was nothing beyond the Rhine but a few hamlets without walls, defended by wooden stakes and ditches. We know that Germany before the time of Henry the Fowler had no walled or fortified towns. In a word, all the details of those times are so many fables, and what is worse, tiresome fables.

LIII

OF THE LEGISLATORS WHO HAVE SPOKEN IN THE NAME OF THE GODS

EVERY PROFANE legislator who dared to feign that the Divinity had dictated to him his laws, was a palpable blasphemer, and a traitor; a blasphemer, because he calumniated the gods; a traitor, because he subjected his country to his own opinions.

There are two sorts of laws, the one natural, common to all, and useful to all. "Thou shalt not steal from, nor shalt thou kill thy neighbor; thou shalt take respectful care of those who gave thee life, and who reared thee in thine infancy; thou shalt not ravish thy brother's wife; thou shalt not lie to prejudice him; thou shalt assist him in his wants, to merit succor from him in turn." Such are the laws which nature has promulgated from the extremity of the islands of Japan to our western coasts. Neither Orpheus, nor Hermes, neither Lycurgus, nor Numa, required Jupiter to appear at the roaring of thunder, to foretell these truths engraven in every heart.

If I had met with one of those great quacks in a public square, I should have called out to him, Stop, do not compromise thus with the Divinity; thou wouldst cheat me, if thou makest him come down to teach us what we all knew; thou wouldst doubtless turn him to some other use;

thou wouldst avail thyself of my agreeing to eternal truths, be but ill-acquainted with the human heart, to suppose it preach thee to the people as a tyrant who blasphemeth.

Other laws are political: laws purely civil and eternally despotic, which at one time establish ephori, at another con-suls, comites by centuries, or comites by tribes, an areopagus or a senate, aristocracy, democracy, or monarchy. We must be but ill acquainted with the human heart, to suppose it could be possible that a profane legislator had ever estab-lished any one of those political laws in the name of the gods, otherwise than with an eye to his own interest. Man are thus deceived only for his emolument.

But have all profane legislators been rogues, deserving of a halter? No: just as it is at present in the assemblies of magistrates. Men of honor and upright principles are always to be met with, who propose things useful to society, with-out boasting that they were revealed to them: so amongst legislators, some have been found who have instituted admir-able laws, without attributing them either to Jupiter or Minerva. Such was the Roman senate, which gave laws to Europe, to little Asia and Africa, without deceiving them; and such in our days was Peter the Great, who might have imposed laws upon his subjects more easily than Hermes did upon the Egyptians, Minos upon the Cretans, or Zamolxis upon the ancient Scythians.